contents

This superb cookbook, richly packed with lovely and immensely useful photographs, will prove to be an invaluable and fascinating addition to any cook's bookshelf. The recipes are clear, easy to follow, beautifully illustrated and temptingly tasty, so whatever your level of expertise in the kitchen you are virtually guaranteed success every time.

Every recipe starts with a photograph of all the ingredients but this is more than just a pretty picture or – even less useful – a montage that is not to scale, so that an orange segment appears the same size as a duck breast. Instead, it serves as an at-a-glance check that you have everything ready before you start cooking. Simply comparing the picture with the ingredients ranged on your own worktop will ensure that you haven't forgotten anything and when it's time to stir in the herbs, for example, you've already chopped them as specified in the ingredients list. If you're not sure how thinly to slice lemon grass or how golden toasted nuts should be, a glance at the photograph will provide an instant answer.

Every short and straightforward step of the method is clearly explained without any jargon or incomprehensible technical terms. Once again, what you see in the photograph is what you should expect to see in your own kitchen. Not only is this reassuring for the beginner, but those with more experience will find it a helpful reminder of the little touches and tricks that can easily be overlooked. Each recipe ends with a mouthwatering photograph of the finished dish, complete with any serving suggestions where relevant.

Why you need this book
This book is the complete answer to the perennial question, 'What shall I cook today?' as it is packed with delicious fuss-free recipes for all occasions, seasons and tastes. Whether you want to rustle up a quick midweek family supper, create a special meal for

guests, prepare a healthy snack, bake a teatime treat or try your hand at something a little more exotic than usual, you are sure to find just the recipes you want. And whether you're a complete novice or a more experienced cook, you're sure of success on a plate.

Buying fresh ingredients

> Not only is seasonal produce less expensive, but as it hasn't had to travel a long distance, it will have a better flavour, texture and colour and retain a higher level of nutrients. Imported fruits and vegetables are often disappointing.

> Root vegetables should be firm with no damp patches. Tomatoes and peppers should have shiny, taut skins. Avoid leafy vegetables with yellowing, discolored, slimy or wilting leaves. Green beans should be crisp enough to snap if you try to bend them.

> Generally speaking, fruit that looks heavy for its size, is firm and unwrinkled will be fresh. Soft fruits should look dry and plump with no signs of mould or wetness. A ripe melon and pineapple should smell fragrant and give slightly when gently pressed.

> Look for fish with a firm body, tight-fitting scales, unfading colours, red gills and full bright eyes. It should have a pleasant, not fishy smell.

Fish and shellfish deteriorate rapidly so are best eaten on the day of purchase. If necessary, they can be kept in the refrigerator for 1 day.

> Meat and poultry should look appetizing and smell pleasant. Depending on the type of meat, the colour will be in the pale pink to red range; it should never look grey. Remember that good-quality mature beef is a dull, dark red. Any fat should be creamy white, not yellow, and waxy, not slimy.

> Keep an eye on the use-by dates on dairy produce, eggs and processed meats such as bacon.

Useful storecupboard stand-bys

Canned goods Canned tomatoes feature in many recipes from casseroles to pasta sauces and are often a much better option than fresh ones, especially out of season or during a poor summer. Canned pulses, such as chickpeas and beans, are convenient but more expensive than dried pulses which require overnight soaking and long cooking.

Dried pasta is the busy cook's best friend. It has a very long shelf life and takes very little time to cook. It's therefore worth having a selection of different shapes, including at least one long variety such as spaghetti or tagliatelle.

Flour Plain flour is used for all kinds of purposes – making pastry, mixing pancakes, thickening sauces. Self-raising flour is used for cakes, scones and dumplings. Adding 2½ teaspoons of baking powder to every 250 g/9 oz of plain flour makes an adequate substitute for self-raising flour if you run out. However, it is always best to use the flour specified in the recipe.

Herbs and spices Fresh herbs are almost always more aromatic and flavoursome than dried and some delicate herbs, such as parsley and basil, are really not suitable for drying. However a stock of more robust dried herbs, such as rosemary and bay leaves, is invaluable. Buy both dried herbs and ground spices in fairly small quantities as they quickly lose their aroma and flavour. Store for up to 3 months in a cool, dark place. Cardamom, coriander, cumin, fennel seeds and peppercorns are best bought whole and freshly ground when needed and they also last a little longer.

Oils Olive oil is full of flavour and ideal for salad dressings and special dishes. It is quite expensive so it is sensible to have a cheaper bland variety, such as sunflower or groundnut, for everyday cooking. Store in a cool, dark place to prevent oils from quickly turning rancid. Don't spend money on expensive nut oils if you're going to use them only once.

Rice Long grain rice is a useful staple. However if you want to make a successful risotto, you will need an Italian rice such as Arborio or Vialone Nano.

Vinegar White wine vinegar is a useful all-round ingredient. Red wine and cider vinegar are also multi-purpose. Balsamic vinegar, now very fashionable, is much more expensive and should be used sparingly. You can make you own herb vinegars by steeping a small bunch of herbs, such as tarragon or thyme, in a bottle of white wine vinegar.

meat

beef stew

serves 4

ingredients

1.3 kg/3 lb boneless braising steak, cut into 5-cm/2-inch pieces
2 tbsp vegetable oil
2 onions, cut into 2.5-cm/1-inch pieces

3 tbsp plain flour
3 garlic cloves, finely chopped
1 litre/1¾ pints beef stock
3 carrots, cut into 2.5-cm/1-inch lengths

2 celery sticks, cut into 2.5-cm/1-inch lengths
1 tbsp tomato ketchup
1 bay leaf
¼ tsp dried thyme
¼ tsp dried rosemary

900 g/2 lb Maris Piper potatoes, cut into large chunks
salt and pepper

>1 Season the steak very generously with salt and pepper. Heat the oil in a large, flameproof casserole over a high heat.

>2 When the oil begins to smoke, add the steak and cook, stirring frequently, for 5–8 minutes, until well browned. Using a slotted spoon, transfer to a bowl.

>3 Reduce the heat to medium, add the onions to the casserole and cook, stirring occasionally, for 5 minutes until translucent.

>4 Stir in the flour and cook, stirring constantly, for 2 minutes. Add the garlic and cook for 1 minute.

> **5** Whisk in 225 ml/8 fl oz of the stock and cook, scraping up all the sediment from the base of the casserole.

> **6** Stir in the remaining stock and add the carrots, celery, tomato ketchup, bay leaf, thyme, rosemary and 1 teaspoon of salt. Return the steak to the casserole.

> **7** Bring back to a gentle simmer, cover and cook over a low heat for 1 hour. Add the potatoes, re-cover the casserole and simmer for a further 30 minutes.

> **8** Remove the lid, increase the heat to medium and cook, stirring occasionally, for a further 30 minutes, or until the meat and vegetables are tender. If the stew becomes too thick, add a little more stock or water. Remove and discard the bay leaf.

Leave to stand for 15 minutes before serving.

meatballs with pepper & tomato sauce

serves 4

ingredients

1 tbsp olive oil
1 small onion, finely
  chopped
2 garlic cloves, finely
  chopped
2 fresh thyme sprigs, finely
  chopped

650 g/1 lb 7 oz fresh beef
  mince
25 g/1 oz fresh
  breadcrumbs
1 egg, lightly beaten
salt and pepper

sauce

1 onion, cut into wedges
3 red peppers, halved and
  deseeded
400 g/14 oz canned
  chopped tomatoes
1 bay leaf
salt and pepper

>**1** Heat the oil in a frying pan. Add the onion and garlic and cook over a low heat for 5 minutes until soft. Place in a bowl with the thyme, beef, breadcrumbs and egg.

>**2** Season to taste with salt and pepper, mix thoroughly and shape into 20 balls. Heat a large frying pan over a medium–low heat. Add the meatballs and cook, stirring gently, for 15 minutes, until lightly browned.

>**3** Meanwhile, to make the sauce, preheat the grill. Cook the onion wedges and red pepper halves under the preheated grill, turning frequently, for 10 minutes, until the pepper skins are blistered and charred.

>**4** Put the peppers into a polythene bag, tie the top and leave to cool. Set the onion wedges aside. Peel off the pepper skins and roughly chop the flesh.

>5 Put the pepper flesh into a food processor with the onion wedges and tomatoes. Process to a smooth purée and season to taste with salt and pepper.

>6 Pour into a saucepan with the bay leaf and bring to the boil. Reduce the heat and simmer, stirring occasionally, for 10 minutes. Remove and discard the bay leaf.

Serve the sauce immediately with
the meatballs.

beef burgers with basil & chilli

serves 4

ingredients
650 g/1 lb 7 oz fresh
  beef mince
1 red pepper, deseeded
  and finely chopped
1 garlic clove, finely
  chopped
2 small red chillies,
  deseeded and finely
  chopped
1 tbsp chopped fresh basil
½ tsp ground cumin
salt and pepper
fresh basil sprigs, to garnish
hamburger buns, to serve

> **1** Preheat the grill to medium–high. Put the beef, red pepper, garlic, chillies, chopped basil and cumin into a bowl.

> **2** Mix until well combined and season to taste with salt and pepper.

Garnish with basil sprigs and serve immediately in hamburger buns.

 3 Using your hands, form the mixture into 4 burger shapes. Place the burgers under the preheated grill and cook for 5–8 minutes.

4 Turn and cook on the other side for 5–8 minutes, or until cooked through.

lasagne

serves 4

ingredients

2 tbsp olive oil
55 g/2 oz pancetta, chopped
1 onion, chopped
1 garlic clove, finely chopped

225 g/8 oz fresh beef mince
2 celery sticks, chopped
2 carrots, chopped
pinch of sugar
½ tsp dried oregano

400 g/14 oz canned chopped tomatoes
2 tsp Dijon mustard
450 ml/16 fl oz ready-made cheese sauce

225 g/8 oz dried no pre-cook lasagne sheets
115 g/4 oz freshly grated Parmesan cheese, plus extra for sprinkling
salt and pepper

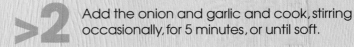

> **1** Preheat the oven to 190°C/375°F/Gas Mark 5. Heat the oil in a large, heavy-based saucepan. Add the pancetta and cook over a medium heat, stirring occasionally, for 3 minutes.

> **2** Add the onion and garlic and cook, stirring occasionally, for 5 minutes, or until soft.

> **3** Add the beef and cook, breaking it up with a wooden spoon, until brown all over. Stir in the celery and carrots and cook for 5 minutes.

> **4** Season to taste with salt and pepper. Add the sugar, oregano and tomatoes and their can juices. Bring to the boil, reduce the heat and simmer for 30 minutes.

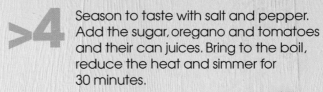

>5 Meanwhile, stir the mustard into the cheese sauce.

>6 In a large, rectangular ovenproof dish, make alternate layers of meat sauce, lasagne sheets and Parmesan cheese.

>7 Pour the cheese sauce over the layers, covering them completely, and sprinkle with Parmesan cheese.

>8 Bake in the preheated oven for 30 minutes, or until golden brown and bubbling.

Serve immediately.

paprika steak wraps with horseradish cream

serves 4

ingredients

4 sirloin steaks, about 175 g/
  6 oz each
1 garlic clove, crushed
2 tsp smoked paprika, plus
  extra for sprinkling
sunflower oil, for brushing
100 g/3½ oz crème fraîche
3 tbsp creamed horseradish
8 small flour tortillas
75 g/2¾ oz rocket leaves
2 firm, ripe avocados,
  peeled, stoned and sliced
1 red onion, thinly sliced
salt and pepper

>1 Spread the steaks with the garlic and sprinkle both sides with the paprika. Season to taste with salt and pepper.

>2 Preheat a ridged griddle pan to very hot and brush with oil. Add the steaks and cook for 6–8 minutes, turning once, or until cooked to your liking. Remove from the heat and leave to rest for 5 minutes.

Serve the wraps with a spoonful of horseradish cream, sprinkled with extra paprika.

>3 Mix together the crème fraîche and horseradish, then spread half over the tortillas.

>4 Slice the steaks into strips. Divide between the tortillas with the rocket, avocado and red onion, wrapping the sides over.

griddled steak with hot chilli salsa

serves 4

ingredients
sunflower oil, for brushing
4 sirloin steaks, about
  225 g/8 oz each
salt and pepper

hot chilli salsa
4 fresh red habanero chillies
4 fresh green poblano
  chillies
3 tomatoes, peeled,
  deseeded and diced

2 tbsp chopped fresh
  coriander
1 tbsp red wine vinegar
2 tbsp olive oil
lamb's lettuce, to garnish

>1 For the salsa, preheat the grill to high. Arrange the chillies on a foil-lined grill pan and cook under the preheated grill, turning frequently, until blackened and charred.

>2 Leave to cool. When cool enough to handle, peel off the skins.

>3 Halve and deseed the chillies, then finely chop the flesh.

>4 Mix together the chillies, tomatoes and coriander in a bowl.

>5 Mix together the vinegar and olive oil in a jug. Season to taste with salt and pour over the salsa. Toss well, cover and chill until required.

>6 Heat a ridged griddle pan over a medium heat and brush lightly with sunflower oil. Season the steaks to taste with salt and pepper, and cook for 2–4 minutes on each side, or until cooked to your liking.

Leave to rest for 3 minutes, then serve with the salsa, garnished with lambs lettuce.

meatloaf

serves 6–8

ingredients

25 g/1 oz butter
1 tbsp olive oil, plus extra
  for brushing
3 garlic cloves, finely
  chopped
100 g/3½ oz carrots, very
  finely diced
55 g/2 oz celery, very finely
  diced

1 onion, very finely diced
1 red pepper, deseeded
  and very finely diced
4 large white mushrooms,
  very finely diced
1 tsp dried thyme
2 tsp finely chopped
  rosemary

1 tsp Worcestershire sauce
6 tbsp tomato ketchup
½ tsp cayenne pepper
1.1 kg/2 lb 8 oz beef mince,
  chilled
2 eggs, beaten
55 g/2 oz fresh
  breadcrumbs

2 tbsp brown sugar
1 tbsp Dijon mustard
salt and pepper

> **1** Melt the butter with the oil and garlic in a large frying pan. Add the vegetables and cook over a medium heat, stirring frequently, for 10 minutes until most of the moisture has evaporated.

> **2** Remove from the heat and stir in the herbs, Worcestershire sauce, 4 tablespoons of tomato ketchup and cayenne pepper. Leave to cool.

> **3** Preheat the oven to 160°C/325°F/ Gas Mark 3. Brush a loaf tin with oil.

> **4** Put the beef into a large bowl and gently break it up with your fingertips. Add the vegetable mixture, eggs and salt and pepper to taste and mix gently with your fingers. Add the breadcrumbs and mix.

5 Transfer the meatloaf mixture to the loaf tin. Smooth the surface and bake in the preheated oven for 30 minutes.

 6 Meanwhile, make a glaze by whisking together the sugar, the remaining 2 tablespoons of tomato ketchup, mustard and a pinch of salt.

7 Remove the meatloaf from the oven and spread the glaze evenly over the top. Return to the oven and bake for a further 35–45 minutes until cooked through and the meat is no longer pink.

8 Remove from the oven and leave to rest for at least 15 minutes.

Slice thickly to serve.

pot roast with potatoes & dill

serves 6

ingredients

4-5 potatoes, unpeeled and cut into chunks
2½ tbsp plain flour
1 tsp salt
¼ tsp pepper

1 rolled brisket joint, weighing 1.6 kg/3 lb 8 oz
2 tbsp vegetable oil
2 tbsp butter
1 onion, finely chopped

2 celery sticks, diced
2 carrots, diced
1 tsp dill seed
1 tsp dried thyme or oregano

350 ml/12 fl oz red wine
150–225 ml/5–8 fl oz beef stock
2 tbsp chopped fresh dill, to serve

> **1** Bring a large saucepan of lightly salted water to the boil. Add the potatoes, bring back to the boil and cook for 10 minutes. Drain and set aside.

> **2** Preheat the oven to 140°C/275°F/ Gas Mark 1. Mix 2 tablespoons of the flour with the salt and pepper in a large shallow dish. Dip the meat in the flour to coat.

> **3** Heat the oil in a flameproof casserole, add the meat and brown. Transfer to a plate. Add half the butter to the casserole, then add the onion, celery, carrots, dill seed and thyme and cook for 5 minutes.

> **4** Return the meat and juices to the casserole. Pour in the wine and enough stock to reach one third of the way up the meat and bring to the boil.

35

> 5 Cover and cook in the oven for 3 hours, turning the meat every 30 minutes. Add the potatoes and more stock, if necessary, after 2 hours.

> 6 When ready, transfer the meat and vegetables to a warmed serving dish. Strain the cooking liquid to remove any solids, then return the liquid to the casserole.

> 7 Mix the remaining butter and flour to a paste.

> 8 Bring the cooking liquid to the boil. Whisk in small pieces of the flour and butter paste, whisking constantly until the sauce is smooth.

Pour the sauce over the meat and vegetables. Sprinkle with fresh dill and serve.

tagliatelle with a rich meat sauce

serves 4

ingredients

4 tbsp olive oil, plus extra
  for drizzling
85 g/3 oz pancetta or
  streaky bacon, diced
1 onion, chopped

1 garlic clove, finely
  chopped
1 carrot, chopped
1 celery stick, chopped
225 g/8 oz fresh beef mince

115 g/4 oz chickens' livers,
  chopped
2 tbsp passata
125 ml/4 fl oz dry white
  wine
225 ml/8 fl oz beef stock

1 tbsp chopped fresh
  oregano
1 bay leaf
450 g/1 lb dried tagliatelle
salt and pepper
grated Parmesan cheese,
  to serve

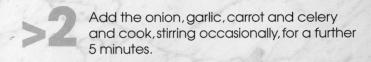

> **1** Heat the oil in a large heavy-based saucepan. Add the pancetta and cook over a medium heat, stirring occasionally, for 3–5 minutes, until it is just turning brown.

> **2** Add the onion, garlic, carrot and celery and cook, stirring occasionally, for a further 5 minutes.

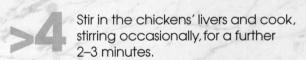

> **3** Add the beef and cook over a high heat, breaking up the meat with a wooden spoon, for 5 minutes, until browned.

> **4** Stir in the chickens' livers and cook, stirring occasionally, for a further 2–3 minutes.

>5 Add the passata, wine, stock, oregano and bay leaf and season to taste with salt and pepper. Bring to the boil, reduce the heat, cover and simmer for 30–35 minutes.

>6 Meanwhile, bring a large saucepan of lightly salted water to the boil. Add the pasta, bring back to the boil and cook for 8–10 minutes, until tender but still firm to the bite.

>7 Drain the pasta and transfer to a warmed serving dish. Drizzle with a little oil and toss well.

>8 Remove and discard the bay leaf from the sauce, then pour the sauce over the pasta and toss again.

Serve immediately with grated Parmesan.

burritos

serves 4

ingredients

1 tbsp olive oil
1 onion, chopped
1 garlic clove, finely
  chopped
500 g/1 lb 2 oz lean fresh
  beef mince

3 large tomatoes,
  deseeded and chopped
1 red pepper, deseeded
  and chopped
800 g/1 lb 12 oz canned
  mixed beans, drained

125 ml/4 fl oz vegetable
  stock
1 tbsp finely chopped fresh
  parsley
8 wholemeal flour tortillas
125 ml/4 fl oz passata

50 g/1¾ oz Cheddar
  cheese, grated
3 spring onions, sliced
sea salt and pepper
mixed salad leaves, to serve

>1 Heat the oil in a large, non-stick frying pan, add the onion and garlic and cook until the onion is soft but not brown. Remove from the pan.

>2 Add the mince and cook over a high heat, breaking it up with a wooden spoon, for 3–4 minutes until beginning to brown. Drain off any excess oil.

>3 Return the onion and garlic to the pan, add the tomatoes and red pepper and cook for 8–10 minutes.

>4 Add the beans, stock and parsley, season to taste with salt and pepper and cook, uncovered, for a further 20–30 minutes until well thickened.

43

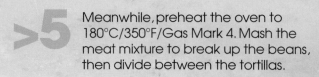 **>5** Meanwhile, preheat the oven to 180°C/350°F/Gas Mark 4. Mash the meat mixture to break up the beans, then divide between the tortillas.

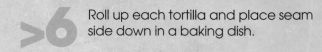 **>6** Roll up each tortilla and place seam side down in a baking dish.

>7 Pour the passata over the burritos and sprinkle over the cheese. Bake in the preheated oven for 20 minutes.

>8 Remove from the oven and scatter over the spring onions.

Transfer to a serving dish and serve with mixed
salad leaves.

beef chop suey

serves 4

ingredients

450 g/1 lb ribeye steak, sliced
1 head broccoli, cut into florets
2 tbsp vegetable oil
1 onion, sliced
2 sticks celery, sliced
225 g/8 oz mangetout, sliced
  lengthways
55 g/2 oz canned bamboo
  shoots, rinsed and shredded
8 water chestnuts, sliced
225 g/8 oz mushrooms, sliced
1 tbsp oyster sauce
1 tsp salt

marinade

1 tbsp Chinese rice wine
½ tsp white pepper
½ tsp salt
1 tbsp light soy sauce
½ tsp sesame oil

> **>1** Combine all the marinade ingredients in a bowl, and marinate the beef for at least 20 minutes.

> **>2** Blanch the broccoli in a large saucepan of boiling water for 30 seconds. Drain and set aside.

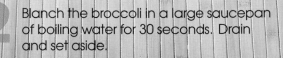

Transfer to bowls and serve immediately.

>3 In a preheated wok, heat 1 tablespoon of the oil and stir-fry the beef until the colour has changed. Remove and set aside.

>4 Clean the wok, heat the remaining oil and stir-fry the onion for 1 minute. Add the celery and broccoli and cook for 2 minutes, Add the mangetout, bamboo shoots, water chestnuts and mushrooms and cook for 1 minute. Add the beef and season with the oyster sauce and salt.

ho fun noodles with beef strips

serves 4

ingredients

300 g/10½ oz rump or sirloin
  beef
2 tbsp soy sauce
2 tbsp sesame oil

250 g/9 oz flat rice noodles
2 tbsp groundnut oil
1 onion, sliced into thin
  wedges

2 garlic cloves, crushed
2.5-cm/1-inch piece fresh
  ginger, chopped
1 red chilli, thinly sliced

200 g/7 oz sprouting
  broccoli
½ Chinese cabbage, sliced
chilli oil, to serve

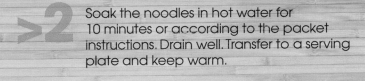

> **1** Slice the beef into thin strips, place in a bowl and sprinkle with soy sauce and sesame oil. Cover and leave to stand for 15 minutes.

> **2** Soak the noodles in hot water for 10 minutes or according to the packet instructions. Drain well. Transfer to a serving plate and keep warm.

> **3** Heat 1 tablespoon of groundnut oil in a wok and stir-fry the beef on a high heat until evenly coloured. Remove and keep to one side.

> **4** Add the remaining oil and stir-fry the onion, garlic, ginger and chilli for 1 minute.

49

>5 Add the broccoli and stir-fry for 2 minutes, then add the cabbage and stir-fry for 1 minute.

>6 Add the beef with any marinade juices and stir until thoroughly heated, then spoon onto the noodles.

Serve immediately, drizzled with chilli oil.

sliced beef in black bean sauce

serves 4

ingredients
3 tbsp groundnut oil
450 g/1 lb beef sirloin, thinly
 sliced
1 red pepper, deseeded
 and thinly sliced
1 green pepper, deseeded
 and thinly sliced
1 bunch spring onions, sliced
2 garlic cloves, crushed
1 tbsp grated fresh ginger
2 tbsp black bean sauce
1 tbsp sherry
1 tbsp soy sauce

>1 Heat 2 tablespoons of the oil in a wok and add the beef. Stir-fry over a high heat for 1–2 minutes. Remove and keep to one side.

>2 Add the remaining oil and peppers and stir-fry for 2 minutes.

Transfer to bowls and serve.

> **>3** Add the spring onions, garlic and ginger and stir-fry for 30 seconds.

> **>4** Add the black bean sauce, sherry and soy sauce, then stir in the beef and heat until bubbling.

teriyaki steak

serves 4

ingredients

4 beef steaks, about 150 g/
5½ oz each
2 tbsp vegetable oil
200 g/7 oz fresh beansprouts

4 spring onions, trimmed
and finely sliced
salt and pepper

teriyaki sauce

2 tbsp mirin (Japanese
rice wine)
2 tbsp sake or pale dry
sherry

4 tbsp dark soy sauce
1 tsp granulated or caster
sugar

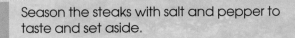

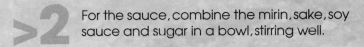

>2 For the sauce, combine the mirin, sake, soy sauce and sugar in a bowl, stirring well.

>3 Heat 1 tablespoon of the oil in a frying pan over a high heat. Add the beansprouts and fry quickly, tossing in the hot oil for 30 seconds.

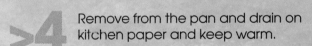

>4 Remove from the pan and drain on kitchen paper and keep warm.

5 Add the remaining oil to the pan and, when hot, add the steaks. Cook for 1–3 minutes on each side, or until cooked to your liking. Remove from the pan and keep warm.

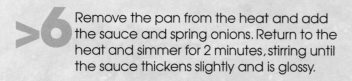**6** Remove the pan from the heat and add the sauce and spring onions. Return to the heat and simmer for 2 minutes, stirring until the sauce thickens slightly and is glossy.

Slice each steak and arrange on a bed of beansprouts. Spoon over the sauce and serve immediately.

risotto with parma ham

serves 4

ingredients

1 tbsp olive oil
25 g/1 oz butter
1 large onion, finely
 chopped
350 g/12 oz risotto rice
about 15 saffron threads
150 ml/5 fl oz white wine
850 ml/1½ pints chicken
 stock
8 sun-dried tomatoes in
 olive oil, drained and
 cut into strips
100 g/3½ oz frozen peas,
 thawed
50 g/1¾ oz Parma ham,
 shredded
75 g/2¾ oz freshly grated
 Parmesan cheese, plus
 extra shavings to serve
salt and pepper

>**1** Heat the oil and butter in a deep saucepan over a medium heat until the butter has melted. Add the onion and cook for 5 minutes until the onion is soft.

>**2** Reduce the heat, add the rice and saffron and mix to coat. Cook, stirring constantly, for 2–3 minutes until the grains are translucent. Add the wine and cook, stirring constantly, until reduced.

Spoon onto warmed plates, sprinkle with Parmesan cheese shavings and serve immediately.

>3 Gradually add the hot stock, a ladleful at a time. Stir constantly, adding more liquid as the rice absorbs each addition. Cook for 10 minutes, then stir in the tomatoes.

>4 Cook for a further 8 minutes, then add the peas and ham. Stir and cook for a further 2–3 minutes, or until all the liquid is absorbed and the rice is creamy but still firm to the bite. Remove from the heat, season to taste and stir in the cheese.

pork chops with apple sauce

serves 4

ingredients

4 pork rib chops on the
  bone, each about
  3 cm/1¼ inches thick,
  at room temperature
1½ tbsp sunflower oil
salt and pepper

apple sauce

450 g/1 lb cooking apples,
  peeled, cored and diced
4 tbsp caster sugar
finely grated zest of
  ½ lemon
½ tbsp lemon juice
4 tbsp water
¼ tsp ground cinnamon
knob of butter

> **1** Preheat the oven to 200°C/400°F/
> Gas Mark 6. To make the apple sauce,
> put the first five ingredients into a heavy-
> based saucepan over a high heat and
> bring to the boil, stirring.

> **2** Reduce the heat to low, cover and
> simmer for 15–20 minutes, until the
> apples are soft. Add the cinnamon
> and butter and beat until you have the
> desired consistency. Remove from the
> heat, cover and keep warm.

Transfer the chops to warmed plates and spoon over the pan juices. Serve immediately, with the apple sauce.

>3 Meanwhile, season the chops to taste with salt and pepper. Heat the oil in a large ovenproof frying pan over a medium–high heat. Add the chops and fry for 3 minutes on each side.

>4 Transfer the pan to the preheated oven and roast the chops for 7–9 minutes until cooked through and the juices run clear when you cut into them. Remove from the oven, cover with foil and leave to stand for 3 minutes.

chorizo, chilli & chickpea casserole

serves 4

ingredients

2 tbsp olive oil
1 onion, sliced
1 large yellow pepper,
  deseeded and sliced
1 garlic clove, crushed

1 tsp chilli flakes
225 g/8 oz chorizo sausage
400 g/14 oz canned
  chopped tomatoes

400 g/14 oz canned
  chickpeas, drained
200 g/7 oz basmati rice
handful of rocket leaves

salt and pepper
4 tbsp roughly chopped
  fresh basil, to garnish

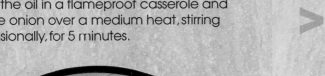

>1 Heat the oil in a flameproof casserole and fry the onion over a medium heat, stirring occasionally, for 5 minutes.

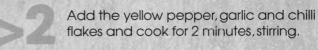

>2 Add the yellow pepper, garlic and chilli flakes and cook for 2 minutes, stirring.

>3 Chop the chorizo into bite-sized chunks and stir into the casserole.

>4 Add the tomatoes and chickpeas with salt and pepper to taste. Bring to the boil, cover and simmer for 10 minutes.

Meanwhile, cook the rice in a saucepan of lightly salted boiling water for 10–12 minutes, until tender. Drain.

>6

Stir the rocket into the casserole.

Serve spooned over the rice, garnished with fresh basil.

pork & rosemary burgers

serves 4

ingredients

500 g/1 lb 2 oz fresh pork
  mince
1 small onion, finely
  chopped
1 garlic clove, crushed
1 tbsp finely chopped fresh
  rosemary
oil, for brushing
1 small French baguette,
  split and cut into four
2 tomatoes, sliced
4 gherkins, sliced
4 tbsp Greek-style yogurt
2 tbsp chopped fresh mint
salt and pepper

>1 Use your hands to mix together the pork, onion, garlic and rosemary with salt and pepper to taste.

>2 Divide the mixture into four and shape into flat burger shapes.

Spoon the minty yogurt over the burgers and replace the baguette tops to serve.

>3 Brush a ridged griddle pan or frying pan with oil and cook the burgers for 6–8 minutes, turning once, until golden and cooked through.

>4 Place a burger on the bottom half of each piece of baguette and top with the tomatoes and gherkins. Mix together the yogurt and mint.

pad noodles with pork strips & prawns

serves 4

ingredients

250 g/9 oz flat rice noodles
200 g/7 oz pork fillet
3 tbsp groundnut oil
2 shallots, finely chopped
2 garlic cloves, finely
 chopped

175 g/6 oz raw prawns,
 peeled and deveined
2 eggs, beaten
2 tbsp Thai fish sauce
juice of 1 lime

1 tbsp tomato ketchup
2 tsp light muscovado sugar
½ tsp dried chilli flakes
100 g/3½ oz beansprouts

4 tbsp roasted salted
 peanuts, chopped
6 spring onions, diagonally
 sliced

> **1** Soak the noodles in hot water for 10 minutes, or according to the packet instructions. Drain well.

> **2** Slice the pork into strips about 5 mm/¼ inch thick.

> **3** Heat the oil in a wok and stir-fry the shallots for 1–2 minutes, to soften.

> **4** Add the pork strips and stir-fry for 2–3 minutes.

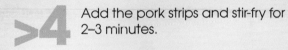

>5 Add the garlic and prawns and stir-fry for 1–2 minutes.

>6 Pour in the beaten eggs and stir for a few seconds until lightly set.

>7 Reduce the heat and add the noodles, fish sauce, lime juice, ketchup and sugar. Toss together and heat through.

>8 Sprinkle with chilli flakes, beansprouts, peanuts and spring onions.

Transfer to bowls and serve.

pork in plum sauce

serves 4

ingredients

600 g/1 lb 5 oz pork fillet
2 tbsp groundnut oil
1 orange pepper,
  deseeded and sliced

1 bunch spring onions, sliced
250 g/9 oz oyster
  mushrooms, sliced
300 g/10½ oz fresh
  beansprouts

2 tbsp dry sherry
150 ml/5 fl oz plum sauce
250 g/9 oz medium egg
  noodles

salt and pepper
chopped fresh coriander,
  to garnish

> **1** Slice the pork into long, thin strips.

> **2** Heat the oil in a wok and stir-fry the pork for 2–3 minutes.

> **3** Add the orange pepper and stir-fry for 2 minutes, then add the spring onions, mushrooms and beansprouts.

> **4** Stir-fry for 2–3 minutes, then add the sherry and plum sauce and heat until boiling. Season well with salt and pepper.

>5 Meanwhile, cook the noodles in a saucepan of lightly salted boiling water for 4 minutes, until tender.

>6 Drain the noodles, then add to the wok and toss well.

Serve immediately, garnished with fresh
coriander.

pork with borlotti beans

serves 4

ingredients

250 g/9 oz dried borlotti
  beans, soaked overnight
800 g/1 lb 12 oz pork shoulder
1 large onion, chopped
2 celery sticks, chopped
1 large carrot, chopped
1 fresh red chilli, finely
  chopped
2 garlic cloves, finely
  chopped
large sprig of each fresh
  rosemary, thyme and bay
  leaves
about 600 ml/1 pint chicken
  stock
salt and pepper
crusty bread, to serve

>1 Preheat the oven to 160°C/325°F/Gas Mark 3. Drain the beans and cook in a saucepan of boiling water for 10 minutes. Drain and tip into a wide ovenproof casserole.

>2 Cut the pork into bite-sized chunks, leaving on any skin.

Serve the pork and beans with chunks of bread to soak up the juices.

 Layer the pork and vegetables over the beans, sprinkling the layers with the chilli, garlic and salt and pepper to taste. Tuck in the herb sprigs.

 Pour over just enough stock to cover, then cover and bake in the preheated oven, without stirring, for 3 hours, until tender.

honeyed apricot lamb with lemon couscous

serves 4

ingredients

4 lamb leg steaks
4 tsp ground coriander
1 tbsp ground cumin

1 small butternut squash
1 tbsp olive oil
1 onion, chopped
600 ml/1 pint chicken stock
2 tbsp chopped fresh ginger

100 g/3½ oz ready-to-eat
   dried apricots
2 tbsp clear honey
finely grated rind and juice
   of 1 lemon

200 g/7 oz couscous
salt and pepper
3 tbsp chopped fresh mint,
   to garnish

>1 Sprinkle the lamb steaks with the ground coriander and cumin.

>2 Peel and deseed the squash and cut into bite-sized chunks.

>3 Heat the oil in a flameproof casserole. Add the lamb and cook over a high heat for 2–3 minutes, turning once.

>4 Stir in the squash, onion and half the stock, then bring to the boil.

>5 Add the ginger, apricots, honey and lemon juice and season to taste with salt and pepper. Cover and cook over a medium heat for about 20 minutes, stirring occasionally.

>6 Meanwhile, bring the remaining stock to the boil in a small saucepan, then stir in the couscous and lemon rind with salt and pepper to taste. Remove from the heat, cover and leave to stand for 5 minutes.

Serve the lamb with the couscous, sprinkled
with fresh mint.

orange & lemon crispy lamb cutlets

serves 2

ingredients
1 garlic clove, crushed
1 tbsp olive oil
2 tbsp finely grated orange
 rind
2 tbsp finely grated lemon
 rind
6 lamb cutlets
salt and pepper
orange wedges, to garnish

>**1** Preheat a ridged griddle pan.

>**2** Mix together the garlic, oil and citrus rinds in a bowl and season to taste with salt and pepper.

Garnish with orange wedges and serve.

>3 Brush the mixture over the lamb cutlets.

>4 Cook the cutlets in the preheated griddle pan for 4–5 minutes on each side.

poultry

chicken noodle soup

serves 4–6

ingredients

2 skinless chicken breasts
2 litres/3½ pints water
1 onion, with skin left on,
  cut in half
1 large garlic clove,
  cut in half

1-cm/½-inch piece fresh
  ginger, peeled and sliced
4 black peppercorns, lightly
  crushed
4 cloves
2 star anise

1 celery stick, chopped
100 g/3½ oz baby corn
  cobs, sliced
2 spring onions, finely
  shredded
115 g/4 oz dried rice
  vermicelli noodles

1 carrot, peeled and
  coarsely grated
salt and pepper

> **1** Put the chicken breasts and water into a saucepan and bring to the boil. Reduce the heat and simmer, skimming the surface until no more foam rises.

> **2** Add the onion, garlic, ginger, peppercorns, cloves, star anise and a pinch of salt.

> **3** Continue to simmer for 20 minutes, or until the chicken is tender and the juices run clear when a skewer is inserted into the thickest part of the meat.

> **4** Remove the chicken and set aside about 1.2 litres/2 pints of stock. Add the celery, baby corn cobs and spring onions.

>5 Bring the stock to the boil and boil until the baby corn cobs are almost tender, then add the noodles and continue boiling for 2 minutes.

>6 Meanwhile, chop the chicken, add to the pan with the grated carrot and continue cooking for about 1 minute, until the chicken is re-heated and the noodles are soft. Add seasoning to taste.

Transfer to bowls and serve.

cream of chicken soup

serves 4

ingredients

3 tbsp butter
4 shallots, chopped
1 leek, sliced
450 g/1 lb skinless chicken
  breasts, chopped

600 ml/1 pint chicken stock
1 tbsp chopped fresh
  parsley
1 tbsp chopped fresh
  thyme, plus extra sprigs
  to garnish

175 ml/6 fl oz double cream
salt and pepper

> **1** Melt the butter in a large saucepan over a medium heat. Add the shallots and cook, stirring, for 3 minutes, until slightly softened.

> **2** Add the leek and cook for a further 5 minutes, stirring.

> **3** Add the chicken, stock and herbs, and season to taste with salt and pepper. Bring to the boil, then reduce the heat and simmer for 25 minutes, until the chicken is tender and cooked through.

> **4** Remove from the heat and leave to cool for 10 minutes. Transfer the soup to a food processor or blender and process until smooth (you may need to do this in batches).

>5

Return the soup to the rinsed-out pan and
warm over a low heat for 5 minutes.

Stir in the cream and cook for a further
2 minutes, then remove from the heat and
ladle into serving bowls.

Garnish with thyme sprigs and serve
immediately.

sticky ginger & soy chicken wings

serves 4

ingredients
12 chicken wings
2 garlic cloves, crushed
2.5-cm/1-inch piece fresh
  ginger, chopped
2 tbsp dark soy sauce
2 tbsp lime juice
1 tbsp clear honey
1 tsp chilli sauce
2 tsp sesame oil
lime wedges, to serve

>1 Tuck the pointed tip of each of the chicken wings under the thicker end to make a neat triangle.

>2 Mix together the garlic, ginger, soy sauce, lime juice, honey, chilli sauce and oil.

Transfer to a serving dish and serve hot, with lime wedges.

>3 Spoon the mixture over the chicken and turn to coat evenly. Cover and marinate for several hours or overnight.

>4 Preheat the grill to hot. Cook the wings on a foil-lined grill pan for 12–15 minutes, or until the chicken is tender and the juices run clear when a skewer is inserted into the thickest part of the meat.

roast chicken with lemon & thyme

serves 6

ingredients

1 chicken, weighing
  2.25 kg/5 lb
55 g/2 oz butter, softened
2 tbsp chopped fresh lemon
  thyme, plus extra sprigs
  to garnish

1 lemon, cut into quarters
125 ml/4 fl oz white wine,
  plus extra if needed
salt and pepper

> 1 Preheat the oven to 220°C/425°F/Gas Mark 7. Place the chicken in a roasting tin.

> 2 Put the butter in a bowl, then mix in the thyme, and salt and pepper to taste and use to butter the chicken.

> 3 Place the lemon inside the cavity. Pour the wine over and roast in the preheated oven for 15 minutes.

> 4 Reduce the temperature to 190°C/375°F/Gas Mark 5 and roast, basting frequently, for a further 1¾ hours.

97

>5 To check a whole bird is cooked through, pierce the thickest part of the leg between the drumstick and the thigh with a thin skewer. Any juices should be piping hot and clear with no traces of red or pink. To further check, gently pull the leg away from the body, the leg should 'give' and no traces of pinkness or blood should remain. Transfer to a warmed platter, cover with foil and allow to rest for 10 minutes.

>6 Place the roasting tin on the hob and simmer the pan juices gently over a low heat until they have reduced and are thick and glossy. Season to taste with salt and pepper and reserve.

>7 To carve the chicken, place on a clean chopping board. Using a carving knife and fork, cut between the wings and the side of the breast. Remove the wings and cut slices off the breast.

>8 Cut the legs from the body and cut through the joint to make drumsticks and thigh portions.

Cut into slices and serve immediately with the gravy, garnished with thyme sprigs.

individual chicken pies

makes 6

ingredients

1 tbsp olive oil
225 g/8 oz button
  mushrooms, sliced
1 onion, finely chopped
350 g/12 oz carrots, sliced
2 celery sticks, sliced

1 litre/1¾ pints cold chicken
  stock
85 g/3 oz butter
55 g/2 oz plain flour, plus
  extra for dusting

900 g/2 lb skinless, boneless
  chicken breasts, cut into
  2.5-cm/1-inch cubes
115 g/4 oz frozen peas
1 tsp chopped fresh thyme

675 g/1 lb 8 oz ready-made
  shortcrust pastry
1 egg, lightly beaten
salt and pepper

> **1** Preheat the oven to 200°C/400°F/Gas Mark 6. Heat the oil in a large saucepan. Add the mushrooms and onion and cook over a medium heat, stirring frequently, for 8 minutes until golden.

> **2** Add the carrots, celery and half the stock and bring to the boil. Reduce the heat to low and simmer for 12–15 minutes until the vegetables are almost tender.

> **3** Meanwhile, melt the butter in a large saucepan over a medium heat. Whisk in the flour and cook, stirring constantly, for 4 minutes.

> **4** Gradually whisk in the remaining stock, then reduce the heat to medium–low and simmer, stirring, until thick. Stir in the vegetable mixture and add the chicken, peas and thyme.

101

>5 Simmer, stirring constantly, for 5 minutes. Taste and adjust the seasoning, adding salt and pepper if needed. Divide the mixture between six large ramekins.

>6 Roll out the pastry on a floured surface and cut out six rounds, each 2.5 cm/ 1 inch larger than the diameter of the ramekins.

>7 Place the pastry rounds on top of the filling, then crimp the edges. Cut a small cross in the centre of each round.

>8 Put the ramekins on a baking sheet and brush the tops with beaten egg. Bake in the preheated oven for 35–40 minutes, until golden brown and bubbling.

Leave to stand for 15 minutes before serving.

chicken fajitas

serves 4

ingredients

3 tbsp olive oil, plus extra
  for drizzling
3 tbsp maple syrup or clear
  honey
1 tbsp red wine vinegar
2 garlic cloves, crushed
2 tsp dried oregano
1–2 tsp dried chilli flakes
4 skinless, boneless chicken
  breasts
2 red peppers, deseeded
  and cut into 2.5-cm/1-inch
  strips
salt and pepper
warmed flour tortillas and
  shredded lettuce, to serve

>1 Place the oil, maple syrup, vinegar, garlic, oregano, chilli flakes, and salt and pepper to taste in a large, shallow dish and mix together.

>2 Slice the chicken across the grain into slices 2.5 cm/1 inch thick. Toss in the marinade to coat. Cover and chill for 2–3 hours, turning occasionally.

Divide the chicken and peppers between the flour tortillas, top with a little shredded lettuce, wrap and serve immediately.

>**3** Drain the chicken, discarding the marinade. Heat a griddle pan until hot. Add the chicken and cook over a medium–high heat for 3–4 minutes on each side until cooked through. Transfer to a warmed plate and keep warm.

>**4** Add the peppers, skin side down, to the pan and cook for 2 minutes on each side until cooked through. Transfer to the plate with the chicken.

chicken wrapped in parma ham with pesto

serves 4

ingredients

4 skinless chicken
  breast fillets
4 tsp green pesto
125 g/4½ oz mozzarella
  cheese

4 thin slices Parma ham
250 g/9 oz cherry plum
  tomatoes, halved
75 ml/2½ fl oz dry white
  wine or chicken stock

1 tbsp olive oil
salt and pepper
fresh ciabatta, to serve

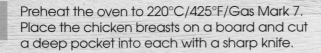 **1** Preheat the oven to 220°C/425°F/Gas Mark 7. Place the chicken breasts on a board and cut a deep pocket into each with a sharp knife.

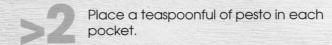 **2** Place a teaspoonful of pesto in each pocket.

3 Cut the cheese into four equal pieces and divide between the chicken breasts, tucking into the pockets.

4 Wrap a slice of ham around each chicken breast to enclose the filling, with the join underneath.

107

>5 Place the chicken in a shallow ovenproof dish and arrange the tomatoes around it.

 >6 Season to taste with salt and pepper, pour over the wine and drizzle with the oil.

 >7 Bake in the preheated oven for 15–20 minutes, until the chicken is tender and the juices run clear when a skewer is inserted into the thickest part of the meat.

>8 Cut the chicken breasts in half diagonally, place on serving plates with the tomatoes and spoon over the juices.

Serve the chicken with chunks of ciabatta on the side.

chicken breasts with a parmesan crumb topping

serves 4

ingredients

4 skinless, boneless chicken breasts
5 tbsp pesto sauce
40 g/1½ oz ciabatta breadcrumbs

25 g/1 oz Parmesan cheese, grated
finely grated rind of ½ lemon
2 tbsp olive oil

salt and pepper
roasted vine tomatoes, to serve

>1 Preheat the oven to 220°C/425°F/Gas Mark 7. Cut a deep slash into each chicken breast to make a pocket.

>2 Open out the chicken breasts and spread 1 tablespoon of the pesto into each pocket.

>3 Fold the chicken flesh back over the pesto and place in an ovenproof dish.

>4 Mix the remaining pesto with the breadcrumbs, Parmesan cheese and lemon rind.

>5 Spread the breadcrumb mixture over the chicken breasts. Season to taste with salt and pepper and drizzle with the oil.

>6 Bake in the preheated oven for about 20 minutes, or until the juices run clear when a skewer is inserted into the thickest part of the meat.

Serve the chicken hot with roasted
vine tomatoes.

steamed chicken with chilli & coriander butter

serves 4

ingredients

55 g/2 oz butter, softened
1 fresh bird's eye chilli,
  deseeded and chopped

3 tbsp chopped fresh
  coriander
4 skinless, boneless chicken
  breasts, about 175 g/6 oz
  each

400 ml/14 fl oz coconut milk
350 ml/12 fl oz chicken stock
200 g/7 oz basmati rice
salt and pepper

pickled vegetables

1 carrot
½ cucumber
3 spring onions
2 tbsp rice vinegar

>1 Mix the butter with the chilli and coriander.

>2 Cut a deep slash into the side of each chicken breast to form a pocket.

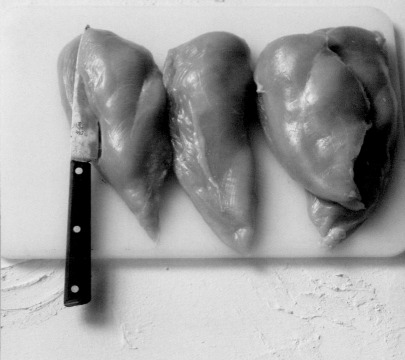

>3 Spoon a quarter of the butter into each pocket and place on a 30-cm/12-inch square of baking paper.

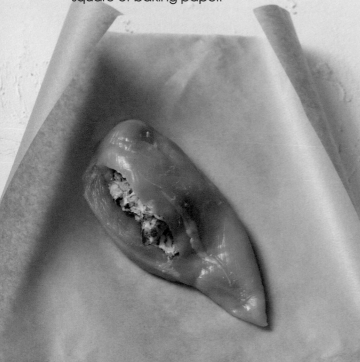

>4 Season to taste with salt and pepper, then bring two opposite sides of the paper together on top, folding over to seal firmly. Twist the ends to seal.

115

>5 Pour the coconut milk and stock into a large saucepan with a steamer top. Bring to the boil. Stir in the rice with a pinch of salt.

>6 Place the chicken parcels in the steamer top, cover and simmer for 15–18 minutes, stirring the rice once, until the rice is tender and the chicken juices run clear when a skewer is inserted into the thickest part of the meat.

>7 Meanwhile, trim the carrot, cucumber and spring onions and cut into fine matchsticks. Sprinkle with the rice vinegar.

>8 Unwrap the chicken, reserving the juices, and cut in half diagonally.

Serve the chicken over the rice, with the juices spooned over and pickled vegetables on the side.

chicken with creamy penne

serves 2

ingredients
200 g/7 oz dried penne
1 tbsp olive oil
2 skinless, boneless chicken
 breasts
4 tbsp dry white wine
115 g/4 oz frozen peas
5 tbsp double cream
salt
4–5 tbsp chopped fresh
 parsley, to garnish

>1 Bring a large saucepan of lightly salted water to the boil. Add the pasta and cook for about 8–10 minutes, until tender but still firm to the bite.

>2 Meanwhile, heat the oil in a frying pan, add the chicken and cook over a medium heat for about 4 minutes on each side.

Garnish with fresh parsley and serve.

>3 Pour in the wine and cook over a high heat until it has almost evaporated and the chicken is tender and the juices run clear when a skewer is inserted into the thickest part of the meat.

>4 Drain the pasta. Add the peas, cream and pasta to the frying pan and stir well. Cover and simmer for 2 minutes.

chicken risotto with saffron

serves 4

ingredients

125 g/4½ oz butter
900 g/2 lb skinless, boneless
  chicken breasts,
  thinly sliced

1 large onion, chopped
500 g/1 lb 2 oz risotto rice
150 ml/5 fl oz white wine
1 tsp crumbled saffron
  threads

1.3 litres/2¼ pints hot
  chicken stock
55 g/2 oz Parmesan cheese,
  grated
salt and pepper

> **1** Heat 55 g/2 oz of the butter in a deep saucepan. Add the chicken and onion and cook, stirring frequently, for 8 minutes, or until golden brown and cooked through.

> **2** Add the rice and mix to coat in the butter. Cook, stirring constantly, for 2–3 minutes, or until the grains are translucent.

> **3** Add the wine and cook, stirring constantly, for 1 minute, until reduced.

> **4** Mix the saffron with 4 tablespoons of the hot stock. Add the liquid to the rice and cook, stirring constantly, until it is absorbed.

>5 Gradually add the remaining hot stock, a ladleful at a time. Add more liquid as the rice absorbs each addition. Cook, stirring, for 20 minutes, or until all the liquid is absorbed and the rice is creamy.

>6 Remove from the heat and add the remaining butter. Mix well, then stir in the Parmesan cheese until it melts. Season to taste with salt and pepper.

Spoon the risotto into warmed serving dishes and serve immediately.

yaki soba

serves 2

ingredients

400 g/14 oz ramen noodles
1 onion, finely sliced
200 g/7 oz beansprouts
1 red pepper, deseeded
   and sliced
150 g/5½ oz chicken,
   cooked and sliced
12 cooked peeled prawns
1 tbsp oil, for stir-frying
2 tbsp shoyu
½ tbsp mirin
1 tsp sesame oil
1 tsp sesame seeds
2 spring onions, finely sliced

> **>1** Cook the noodles according to the packet instructions, drain well, and tip into a bowl.

> **>2** Mix together the onion, beansprouts, red pepper, chicken and prawns in a bowl. Stir through the noodles. Meanwhile, preheat a wok over a high heat, add the oil and heat until very hot.

Sprinkle with sesame seeds and spring onions and serve.

>3 Add the noodle mixture and stir-fry for 4 minutes, or until golden, then add the shoyu, mirin and sesame oil and toss together.

>4 Divide the noodles between two bowls.

chicken with cashew nuts

serves 4–6

ingredients

450 g/1 lb boneless chicken meat, cut into bite-sized pieces

3 tbsp light soy sauce

1 tsp Chinese rice wine
pinch of sugar
½ tsp salt
3 dried Chinese mushrooms, soaked in warm water for 20 minutes

2 tbsp vegetable or groundnut oil
4 slices of fresh ginger
1 tsp finely chopped garlic

1 red pepper, deseeded and cut into 2.5-cm/1-inch squares
85 g/3 oz cashew nuts, toasted

>1 Marinate the chicken in 2 tablespoons of the light soy sauce, Chinese rice wine, sugar and salt for at least 20 minutes.

>2 Squeeze any excess water from the mushrooms and finely slice, discarding any tough stems. Reserve the soaking water.

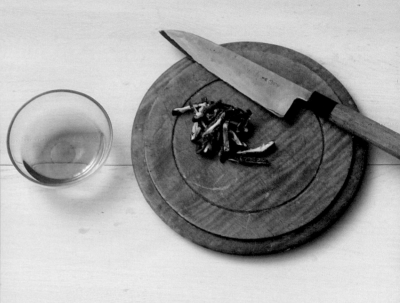

>3 In a preheated wok, heat 1 tablespoon of the oil. Add the ginger and stir-fry until fragrant. Stir in the chicken and cook for 2 minutes, until it turns brown. Before the chicken is cooked through, remove and set aside.

>4 Clean the wok, heat the remaining oil and stir-fry the garlic until fragrant. Add the mushrooms and red pepper and stir-fry for 1 minute.

>5 Add about 2 tablespoons of the mushroom soaking water and cook for about 2 minutes until the water has evaporated.

>6 Return the chicken to the wok, add the remaining light soy sauce and the cashew nuts and stir-fry for 2 minutes until the chicken is cooked through.

green chicken curry

serves 4

ingredients

2 tbsp groundnut or
   vegetable oil
4 spring onions, roughly
   chopped
2 tbsp green curry paste
700 ml/1¼ pints canned
   coconut milk
1 chicken stock cube
6 skinless chicken breasts,
   cut into 2.5-cm/1-inch
   cubes
large handful of fresh
   coriander, chopped
1 tsp salt
cooked rice, to serve

> **>1** Heat the oil in a preheated wok, add the spring onions and stir-fry over a medium–high heat for 30 seconds, or until starting to soften.

> **>2** Add the curry paste, coconut milk and stock cube and bring gently to the boil, stirring occasionally.

Serve immediately with rice.

>3 Add the chicken cubes, half the coriander and the salt and stir well. Reduce the heat and simmer gently for 8–10 minutes until the chicken is cooked through.

>4 Stir in the remaining coriander.

teriyaki chicken

serves 4

ingredients

4 boneless chicken breasts,
   about 175 g/6 oz each,
   with or without skin
4 tbsp bottled teriyaki sauce
   plus extra if needed
peanut or corn oil, for
   brushing

sesame noodles
250 g/9 oz dried thin
   buckwheat noodles
1 tbsp toasted sesame oil
2 tbsp sesame seeds,
   toasted

2 tbsp finely chopped fresh
   parsley
salt and pepper

> **>1** Using a sharp knife score each chicken breast diagonally across 3 times. Rub all over with teriyaki sauce. Set aside in the refrigerator to marinate for at least 10 minutes and up to 24 hours.

> **>2** Meanwhile, to make the sesame noodles, preheat the grill to high. Bring a saucepan of water to the boil, add the buckwheat noodles and cook according to the packet instructions. Drain and rinse well in cold water.

> **>3** Lightly brush the griddle pan with peanut oil. Add the chicken breasts, skin side up, and brush again with a little extra teriyaki sauce.

> **>4** Griddle the chicken breast, brushing occasionally with extra teriyaki sauce, for 15 minutes, or until tender and the juices run clear when a skewer is inserted into the thickest part of the meat.

133

>5 Meanwhile, heat a wok over a high heat. Add the sesame oil and heat until it shimmers.

>6 Add the noodles and stir round to heat through, then stir in the sesame seeds and parsley. Season to taste with salt and pepper.

Transfer the chicken breasts to plates and
serve with the noodles

creamy turkey & broccoli gnocchi

serves 4

ingredients

1 tbsp sunflower oil
500 g/1 lb 2 oz turkey
  stir-fry strips
2 small leeks, sliced
  diagonally
500 g/1 lb 2 oz ready-made
  fresh gnocchi
200 g/7 oz broccoli, cut into
  bite-sized pieces
85 g/3 oz crème fraîche
1 tbsp wholegrain mustard
3 tbsp orange juice
salt and pepper
3 tbsp toasted pine kernels,
  to serve

> **1** Heat the oil in a wok or large frying pan, then add the turkey and leeks and stir-fry over a high heat for 5–6 minutes, until the turkey is cooked through.

> **2** Meanwhile, bring a saucepan of lightly salted water to the boil. Add the gnocchi and broccoli, and cook for 3–4 minutes.

136

Serve immediately, sprinkled with pine kernels.

3 Drain the gnocchi and broccoli and stir into the turkey mixture.

4 Mix together the crème fraîche, mustard and orange juice in a small bowl. Season to taste with salt and pepper, then stir into the wok.

grilled turkey breast with lemon

serves 4

ingredients

1 lemon

2 tbsp olive oil

1 garlic clove, crushed

4 turkey breast steaks

salt and pepper

salad, to serve

> **>1** Finely grate the rind from the lemon and squeeze the juice.

> **>2** Mix together the lemon rind, lemon juice, oil and garlic in a wide, non-metallic dish.

> **>3** Place the turkey steaks in the lemon mixture, turning to coat evenly. Cover with clingfilm and chill in the refrigerator for 30 minutes. Drain the turkey, discarding the marinade.

> **>4** Preheat a griddle pan to hot. Season the turkey steaks with salt and pepper to taste, place in the pan and cook for about 4 minutes, until golden.

Using tongs, turn the turkey steaks over and cook the other side for 3–4 minutes, until the turkey is tender and the juices run clear when a skewer is inserted into the thickest part of the meat.

>6

Transfer the turkey to a warmed plate, cover with foil and leave to stand for 3–4 minutes before serving.

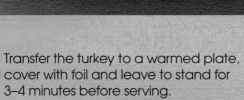

Serve with salad.

turkey schnitzel with potato wedges

serves 4

ingredients

4 potatoes, unpeeled
2 tbsp olive oil, plus extra for shallow frying

1 tbsp dried sage
55 g/2 oz fresh white breadcrumbs

40 g/1½ oz finely grated Parmesan cheese
4 thinly sliced turkey escalopes

1 egg, beaten
salt and pepper
lemon wedges, to serve

> **>1** Preheat the oven to 220°C/425°F/Gas Mark 7. Cut each potato into eight wedges.

> **>2** Place the potato wedges in a bowl and add the oil, 1 teaspoon of the sage, and salt and pepper to taste. Toss well to coat evenly.

> **>3** Arrange the potatoes in a single layer on a baking sheet. Bake in the oven for about 25 minutes, until golden brown and tender.

> **>4** Meanwhile, mix together the breadcrumbs, cheese, remaining sage, and salt and pepper to taste.

>5 Dip the turkey in the beaten egg and then in the crumb mixture, pressing to coat on both sides.

>6 Heat a shallow depth of oil in a frying pan over a fairly high heat, add the turkey and fry for 4–5 minutes, turning once, until golden brown and the turkey is cooked through.

Serve the turkey hot with the potato and
lemon wedges.

turkey stir-fry

serves 4

ingredients

450 g/1 lb turkey breast,
  skinned and cut into strips
200 g/7 oz basmati rice
1 tbsp vegetable oil
1 broccoli stalk,
  cut into florets

2 heads pak choi, washed
  and separated
1 red pepper, thinly sliced
50 ml/2 fl oz chicken stock
salt

marinade

1 tbsp soy sauce
1 tbsp honey
2 garlic cloves, crushed

> **1** To make the marinade, combine the ingredients in a medium-sized bowl. Add the turkey and toss to coat. Cover with clingfilm and marinate in the refrigerator for 2 hours.

> **2** Cook the rice in a saucepan of lightly salted water for 10–12 minutes, until tender. Drain and keep warm.

> **3** Meanwhile, preheat a wok over a medium–high heat, add the oil and heat for 1 minute. Add the turkey and stir-fry for 3 minutes or until the turkey is cooked through.

> **4** Remove the turkey with a slotted spoon, set aside and keep warm. Add the broccoli, pak choi and red pepper to the wok and stir-fry for 2 minutes.

147

>5 Add the stock and continue to stir-fry for 2 minutes, or until the vegetables are tender but still firm to the bite.

>6 Return the turkey to the wok and cook briefly to reheat.

Serve immediately with the rice.

hoisin & sesame-glazed grilled duck

serves 4

ingredients

2 duck breasts,
   about 225 g/8 oz each
½ tsp ground star anise
3 tbsp hoisin sauce
1 tbsp sesame oil
1 ripe mango
½ cucumber
4 spring onions
1 tbsp rice vinegar
toasted sesame seeds,
   to sprinkle

>1 Using a sharp knife, score the skin of the duck breast in a diamond pattern.

>2 Mix the star anise, hoisin sauce and sesame oil and brush over the duck. Cover and marinate for at least 30 minutes.

Serve the duck slices arranged over a spoonful of the mango salad, sprinkled with sesame seeds.

>3 Meanwhile, peel, stone and thinly slice the mango. Cut the cucumber into matchsticks and thinly slice the onions. Stir together and sprinkle with vinegar.

>4 Preheat the grill to hot. Grill the duck for 8–10 minutes on each side, brushing with the marinade. Rest for 5 minutes, then slice thinly.

duck breasts with citrus glaze

serves 4

ingredients

55 g/2 oz light brown sugar,
  plus extra if needed
finely grated rind and juice
  of 1 orange

finely grated rind and juice
  of 1 large lemon
finely grated rind and juice
  of 1 lime
4 duck breasts, skin on

2 tbsp olive oil
salt and pepper
freshly cooked sugar snap
  peas and orange wedges,
  to serve

>1 Put the sugar in a small saucepan, add just enough water to cover and heat gently until dissolved.

>2 Add the citrus rinds and juices and bring to the boil.

>3 Reduce the heat and simmer for about 10 minutes, until syrupy. Remove from the heat. Taste and add extra sugar if needed. Keep warm.

>4 Meanwhile, score the skin of the duck breasts with a sharp knife in a diamond pattern and rub with salt and pepper.

>5 Heat the oil in a frying pan. Place the duck breasts skin-side down in the pan and cook for 5 minutes on each side, until the flesh is just pink.

>6 Slice the duck breasts diagonally into five to six slices and transfer to warmed plates.

Arrange some sugar snap peas and orange wedges on each plate, spoon over the glaze and serve immediately.

fish & seafood

grilled fish with lemon

serves 4

ingredients

olive oil, for brushing
4 white fish steaks or fillets,
   about 175 g/6 oz each

salt and pepper
lemon wedges, to serve

>1
Preheat the grill to very hot. Brush a shallow flameproof dish with oil.

>2
To remove the skin, place the fish skin-side down and slide a sharp knife between the skin and the flesh, keeping the knife flat.

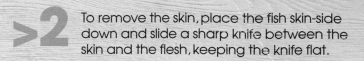

>3
Lay the fish in the prepared dish and brush with oil. Sprinkle with salt and pepper.

>4
Place under the grill and cook for 3–4 minutes until the surface of the fish is firm and white.

>5 Using a fish slice, carefully turn the fillets. Brush with oil and sprinkle with salt and pepper.

>6 Grill the other side for 3–4 minutes, depending on the thickness, until the fish is firm and flakes easily with a fork.

Serve immediately with lemon wedges.

fish goujons with chilli mayonnaise

serves 4

ingredients

200 g/7 oz plain flour
3 eggs
140 g/5 oz matzo meal
450 g/1 lb firm white fish
  fillets, cut into strips

sunflower or groundnut oil,
  for shallow-frying
salt and pepper

chilli mayonnaise

2 tbsp sweet chilli sauce
4–5 tbsp mayonnaise

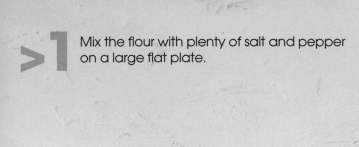

>**1** Mix the flour with plenty of salt and pepper on a large flat plate.

>**2** Beat the eg

>**5** Pou
a

>**3** Spread out the matzo meal on another flat plate.

>**4** Dip the fish pieces into the seasoned flour, then into the beaten egg, then into the matzo meal, ensuring a generous coating.

the oil into a non-stick frying pan to
depth of 1 cm/½ inch and heat. Cook
the fish pieces in batches for a few
minutes, turning once, until golden and
cooked through. Keep the fish goujons
warm while you cook the remainder.

>6 To make the chilli mayonnaise, put the chilli
sauce and mayonnaise in a bowl and
beat together until combined.

Transfer the fish to warmed plates and serve
with the chilli mayonnaise on the side.

peppered tuna steaks

serves 4

ingredients

4 tuna steaks, about 175 g/
  6 oz each
4 tsp sunflower oil or olive oil
1 tsp salt
2 tbsp pink, green and black
  peppercorns, roughly
  crushed
handful of fresh rocket
  leaves, to garnish
lemon wedges, to serve

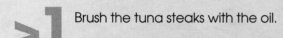

>1 Brush the tuna steaks with the oil.

>2 Sprinkle with the salt.

Garnish with rocket and serve with lemon wedges for squeezing over.

>3 Coat the fish in the crushed peppercorns.

>4 Heat a ridged griddle pan over a medium heat. Add the tuna and cook for 2–3 minutes on each side.

tuna pasta bake

serves 4

ingredients

250 g/9 oz dried elbow
  macaroni
375 g/13 oz canned tuna in
  oil, drained and flaked
1 small red onion, grated
2 tbsp chopped fresh
  parsley
200 g/7 oz Cheddar cheese,
  grated
1 large egg, beaten
225 ml/8 fl oz single cream
¼ tsp grated nutmeg
salt and pepper

>1 Preheat the oven to 220°C/425°F/Gas Mark 7
and place a baking sheet on the middle shelf
to heat. Bring a saucepan of lightly salted
water to the boil, add the macaroni and cook
according to the packet instructions, or until
tender but still firm to the bite. Drain.

>2 Combine the macaroni, tuna, onion,
parsley and half the cheese in a
shallow, 2-litre/3½-pint ovenproof dish,
spreading evenly.

Serve hot.

fish

makes

ingre
300

>3 Beat the egg with the cream, nutmeg, and salt and pepper to taste. Pour over the macaroni mixture and sprinkle with the remaining cheese.

>4 Place the dish on the preheated baking sheet in the oven and bake for about 15 minutes, until golden brown and bubbling.

cakes

...8

...dients

- ...g/10½ oz floury
  potatoes, cut into chunks
- 300 g/10½ oz cooked
  peppered salmon, flaked
- 8 tbsp chopped fresh dill,
  plus extra to garnish
- 6 spring onions, some green
  parts included, finely
  chopped

- 1 tbsp coarsely grated
  lemon zest
- 1 tbsp cornflour, sifted
- 1 tsp salt
- ½ tsp pepper
- 2 eggs, lightly beaten
- flour, for dusting
- oil, for frying

aïoli

- 3 large garlic cloves
- 1 tsp sea salt flakes
- 2 egg yolks, at room
  temperature
- 250 ml/9 fl oz extra virgin
  olive oil
- 2 tbsp lemon juice

> 1 Bring a large saucepan of water to the boil, add the potatoes, bring back to the boil and cook for 20 minutes or until tender. Drain well, mash and set aside.

> 2 Put the salmon, potato, dill, spring onions and lemon zest into a large bowl and lightly mix with a fork.

> 3 Sprinkle with the cornflour, salt and pepper. Stir in the eggs.

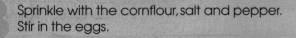

> 4 With floured hands, form the mixture into 8 patties about 2 cm/¾ inch thick.

> 5 Place on a sheet lined with baking paper and chill for at least 2 hours.

> 6 To make the aïoli, use a mortar and pestle to crush the garlic and salt to a smooth paste. Transfer to a large bowl. Beat in the egg yolks.

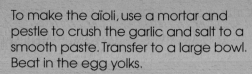

> 7 Add the oil, a few drops at a time, whisking constantly, until thick and smooth. Beat in the lemon juice. Cover with clingfilm and set aside.

> 8 Heat the oil in a frying pan and cook the cakes over a medium–high heat for 8 minutes, until golden. Turn and cook the other side for 4–5 minutes until golden.

Garnish with dill and serve immediately with the aïoli.

steamed salmon

serves 4

ingredients
40 g/1½ oz butter, melted
4 salmon fillets, about
  140 g/5 oz each
finely grated rind and juice
  of 1 lemon
1 tbsp snipped chives
1 tbsp chopped parsley
salt and pepper
salad and crusty bread,
  to serve

> **1** Preheat the oven to 200°/400°F/Gas Mark 6. Cut four 30-cm/12-inch squares of double thickness foil and brush with the melted butter.

> **2** Place a piece of salmon on each square and spoon over the lemon rind and juice. Sprinkle with the chives and parsley and season to taste with salt and pepper.

174

Transfer the salmon and juices to warmed serving plates and serve immediately with salad and crusty bread.

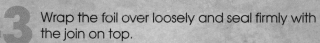
>3 Wrap the foil over loosely and seal firmly with the join on top.

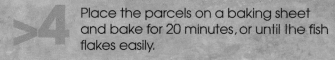
>4 Place the parcels on a baking sheet and bake for 20 minutes, or until the fish flakes easily.

seared sesame salmon with pak choi

serves 4

ingredients

2.5-cm/1-inch piece fresh
ginger
1 tbsp soy sauce

1 tsp sesame oil
4 skinless salmon fillets
2 tbsp sesame seeds
lime wedges, to serve

stir-fry

2 small pak choi
1 bunch spring onions
1 tbsp sunflower oil

1 tsp sesame oil
salt and pepper

>1 Peel and finely grate the ginger and mix with the soy sauce and sesame oil in a shallow dish.

>2 Add the salmon fillets, turning to coat evenly on both sides.

>3 Sprinkle the salmon on one side with half the sesame seeds, then turn and sprinkle the other side with the remaining sesame seeds.

>4 To prepare the stir-fry vegetables, cut the pak choi lengthways into quarters.

>5 Cut the spring onions into thick diagonal slices.

>6 Preheat a heavy-based frying pan. Add the salmon and cook for 3–4 minutes. Turn and cook for a further 3–4 minutes.

>7 Meanwhile, heat the sunflower and sesame oils in a wok, add the pak choi and spring onions and stir-fry for 2–3 minutes. Season to taste with salt and pepper.

>8 Divide the vegetables between warmed serving plates and place the salmon on top.

Serve immediately with lime wedges for squeezing over.

sea bass with olive gremolata

serves 4

ingredients

900 g/2 lb small new
  potatoes, unpeeled
4 sea bass fillets, about
  175 g/6 oz each

1 tbsp olive oil
4 tbsp dry white wine
salt and pepper

olive gremolata

grated rind of 1 lemon
1 garlic clove, chopped
2 large handfuls flat-leaf
  parsley (about 55 g/2 oz)

70 g/2½ oz stoned black
  olives
2 tbsp capers
2 tbsp olive oil

>1 Cook the potatoes in a saucepan of lightly salted boiling water for 15–20 minutes, or until tender.

>2 Meanwhile, make the gremolata. Place the lemon rind, garlic, parsley, olives, capers and oil in a food processor and process briefly to form a rough paste.

>3 Brush the sea bass with the oil and season to taste with salt and pepper. Heat a heavy-based frying pan and fry the sea bass for 5–6 minutes, turning once.

>4 Remove the fish from the pan and keep warm. Stir the wine into the pan and boil for 1 minute, stirring.

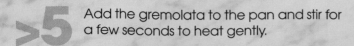

>5 Add the gremolata to the pan and stir for a few seconds to heat gently.

>6 Drain the potatoes when tender and crush lightly with a wooden spoon or potato masher.

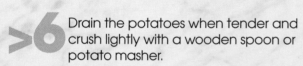

Serve the sea bass and crushed potatoes topped with the gremolata.

monkfish skewers
with basil mayonnaise

serves 2–4

ingredients

1 garlic clove, crushed
finely grated rind and juice
  of 1 lemon
2 tbsp olive oil
500 g/1 lb 2 oz monkfish
  fillet, cut into 3-cm/1¼-inch
  chunks

2 red onions, cut into thin
  wedges
salt and pepper

basil mayonnaise

2 egg yolks
1 tbsp lemon juice
1 tsp Dijon mustard
150 ml/5 fl oz sunflower oil
150 ml/5 fl oz extra virgin
  olive oil

55 g/2 oz fresh basil leaves,
  chopped
salt and pepper

>1 Mix together the garlic, lemon rind and juice and olive oil and add salt and pepper to taste. Stir in the fish, cover and leave to marinate in the refrigerator for 30 minutes.

>2 For the basil mayonnaise, whisk together the egg yolks, lemon juice and mustard until smooth.

>3 Whisk in the sunflower oil until the mixture thickens.

>4 Whisk in the extra virgin olive oil in a thin, steady stream to make a thick, creamy sauce. Stir in the basil and adjust the seasoning, adding salt and pepper if needed.

>5 Preheat the grill to high. Drain the monkfish, reserving the marinade. Thread the monkfish and onion alternately onto 4 metal or pre-soaked wooden skewers.

>6 Cook the skewers under the preheated grill, turning occasionally and basting with the reserved marinade, for 6–8 minutes, until golden.

Serve the skewers hot with the basil mayonnaise.

187

monkfish with a lemon & parsley crust

serves 4

ingredients

4 tbsp sunflower oil
4 tbsp fresh breadcrumbs
4 tbsp chopped fresh
  parsley, plus extra sprigs to
  garnish
finely grated rind of 1 large
  lemon
4 monkfish fillets, about
  140–175 g/5–6 oz each
salt and pepper

>1 Preheat the oven to 180°C/350°F/ Gas Mark 4. Mix together the oil, breadcrumbs, parsley and lemon rind in a bowl until well combined. Season to taste with salt and pepper.

>2 Place the fish fillets in a large roasting tin.

Garnish with parsley sprigs and serve.

3 Divide the breadcrumb mixture between the fish and press it down with your fingers to ensure it covers the fillets.

4 Bake in the preheated oven for 7–8 minutes, or until the fish is cooked through.

rustic fish casserole

serves 4

ingredients

300 g/10½ oz live clams
2 tbsp olive oil
1 large onion, chopped

2 garlic cloves, crushed
2 celery sticks, sliced
350 g/12 oz firm white fish
    fillet

250 g/9 oz prepared squid
    rings
400 ml/14 fl oz fish stock
6 plum tomatoes, chopped

small bunch of fresh thyme
salt and pepper
crusty bread, to serve

>1
Clean the clams under cold running water, scrubbing the shells. Discard any with broken shells and any that refuse to close when tapped.

>2
Heat the oil in a large saucepan and fry the onion, garlic and celery for 3–4 minutes, until softened but not browned.

>3
Meanwhile, cut the fish into chunks.

>4
Stir the fish and squid into the pan, then fry gently for 2 minutes.

>5 Stir in the stock, tomatoes and thyme and season to taste with salt and pepper. Cover and simmer gently for 3–4 minutes.

>6 Add the clams, cover and cook over a high heat for a further 2 minutes, or until the shells open. Discard any that remain closed.

Serve the casserole immediately with chunks of bread.

paella

serves 6–8

ingredients

6 tbsp olive oil
6–8 boned chicken thighs
140 g/5 oz Spanish chorizo
  sausage, sliced
2 large onions, chopped
4 large garlic cloves,
  crushed

1 tsp mild or hot Spanish
  paprika
350 g/12 oz paella rice,
  rinsed and drained
100 g/3½ oz French beans,
  chopped
125 g/4½ oz frozen peas

1.3 litres/2¼ pints fish stock
½ tsp saffron threads,
  soaked in 2 tbsp hot water
16 live mussels, soaked in
  salted water for 10 minutes
16 raw prawns, peeled and
  deveined

2 red peppers, halved and
  deseeded, then grilled,
  peeled and sliced
salt and pepper
freshly chopped parsley,
  to garnish

> **1** Heat 3 tablespoons of the oil in a 30-cm/12-inch paella pan or casserole. Cook the chicken over a medium–high heat, turning frequently, for 5 minutes, or until golden and crisp.

> **2** Using a slotted spoon, transfer to a bowl.

> **3** Add the chorizo to the pan and cook, stirring, for 1 minute, or until beginning to crisp, then add to the chicken.

> **4** Heat the remaining oil in the pan, add the onions and cook, stirring, for 2 minutes.

>5 Add the garlic and paprika and cook for a further 3 minutes, or until the onions are soft but not brown.

>6 Add the rice, beans and peas and stir until coated in oil. Return the chicken and chorizo and any accumulated juices to the pan.

>7 Stir in the stock, saffron and its soaking liquid, and salt and pepper to taste and bring to the boil, stirring. Reduce the heat to low and simmer, uncovered, for 15 minutes.

>8 Discard any mussels with broken shells and any that refuse to close when tapped. Arrange the mussels, prawns and peppers on top. Cover and simmer for 5 minutes until the prawns turn pink and the mussels open. Discard any mussels that remain closed. Ensure the chicken is cooked through.

Garnish with the parsley and serve immediately.

thai prawn noodle bowl

serves 4

ingredients

1 bunch spring onions	2 tbsp groundnut oil	400 ml/14 fl oz fish or	350 g/12 oz cooked peeled
2 celery sticks	55 g/2 oz unsalted peanuts	chicken stock	king prawns
1 red pepper	1 fresh bird's eye chilli, sliced	200 ml/7 fl oz coconut milk	salt and pepper
200 g/7 oz rice vermicelli	1 lemon grass stem, crushed	2 tsp Thai fish sauce	3 tbsp chopped fresh
noodles			coriander, to garnish

>1 Trim the spring onions and celery and thinly slice diagonally. Deseed and thinly slice the pepper.

>2 Place the noodles in a bowl, cover with boiling water and leave to stand for 4 minutes, or until tender. Drain.

>3 Heat the oil in a wok and stir-fry the peanuts for 1–2 minutes, until golden. Lift out with a slotted spoon.

>4 Add the sliced spring onions, celery and red pepper to the wok and stir-fry over a high heat for 1–2 minutes.

>5 Add the chilli, lemon grass, stock, coconut milk and fish sauce and bring to the boil.

>6 Stir in the prawns and bring back to the boil, stirring. Season to taste with salt and pepper, then add the noodles.

Transfer to warmed bowls, garnish with
coriander and serve.

ginger prawns with oyster mushrooms

serves 4

ingredients

150 ml/5 fl oz chicken stock
2 tsp sesame seeds
1 tbsp grated fresh ginger
1 tbsp soy sauce

¼ tsp hot pepper sauce
1 tsp cornflour
3 tbsp vegetable oil
3 carrots, thinly sliced

350 g/12 oz oyster
   mushrooms, thinly slice
1 large red pepper,
   deseeded and thinly sliced

450 g/1 lb raw king prawns,
   peeled and deveined
2 garlic cloves, crushed
fresh coriander sprigs,
   to garnish
freshly cooked rice, to serve

> **1** In a small bowl, stir together the stock, sesame seeds, ginger, soy sauce, hot pepper sauce and cornflour until well blended. Set aside.

> **2** Add 2 tablespoons of the oil to a large wok and heat. Stir-fry the carrots for 3 minutes, remove from the wok and set aside.

> **3** Add the remaining oil to the wok and stir-fry the mushrooms for 2 minutes. Remove from the wok and set aside.

> **4** Add the red pepper, prawns and garlic to the wok and stir-fry for 3 minutes, until the prawns turn pink and start to curl.

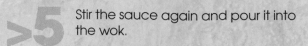

>5 Stir the sauce again and pour it into the wok.

>6 Cook until the mixture bubbles, then return the carrots and mushrooms to the wok. Cover and cook for a further 2 minutes, until heated through.

Garnish with coriander sprigs and serve over cooked rice.

wine-steamed mussels

serves 4

ingredients
115 g/4 oz butter
1 shallot, chopped
3 garlic cloves, finely
  chopped
2 kg/4 lb 8 oz live mussels,
  scrubbed and debearded
225 ml/8 fl oz dry white wine
½ tsp salt
4 tbsp chopped fresh
  parsley
pepper
fresh crusty bread, to serve

>1 Place half the butter in a large saucepan and melt over a low heat. Add the shallot and garlic and cook for 2 minutes.

>2 Discard any mussels with broken shells and any that refuse to close when tapped. Add the mussels and wine to the pan with the salt and pepper to taste. Cover and bring to the boil, then cook for 3 minutes, shaking the pan from time to time.

Serve immediately with fresh crusty bread for mopping up the juices.

>3 Remove the mussels from the pan with a slotted spoon and place in individual serving bowls. Discard any mussels that remain closed.

>4 Stir the remaining butter and the parsley into the cooking juices in the pan. Bring to the boil, then pour over the mussels.

seafood risotto

serves 4

ingredients

150 ml/5 fl oz dry white wine
4 baby squid, cleaned and
    sliced
250 g/9 oz raw prawns,
    peeled and deveined

250 g/9 oz live mussels,
    scrubbed and debearded
2 tbsp olive oil
55 g/2 oz butter
1 onion, finely chopped

2 garlic cloves, finely
    chopped
2 bay leaves
350 g/12 oz risotto rice

about 1.5 litres/2¾ pints
    fish stock
salt and pepper
chopped fresh flat-leaf
    parsley, to garnish

> **>1** Heat the wine in a saucepan until boiling. Add the squid and prawns, cover and cook for 2 minutes. Remove the squid and prawns with a slotted spoon and set aside.

> **>2** Discard any mussels with broken shells and any that refuse to close when tapped. Add the mussels to the pan, cover and cook for 2–3 minutes, until they have opened. Discard any that remain closed. Drain the mussels, reserving the juices, and remove from their shells.

> **>3** Heat the oil and butter in a deep saucepan. Add the onion and cook, stirring frequently, for 3–4 minutes, until softened.

> **>4** Add the garlic, bay leaves and rice, and mix to coat in the butter and oil. Cook, stirring constantly, for 2–3 minutes, until the grains are translucent.

>5 Stir in the cooking juices from the mussels, then gradually add the hot stock, a ladleful at a time. Cook, stirring, for 15 minutes, until the liquid is absorbed and the rice is creamy.

 >6 Stir in the cooked seafood, cover and cook for a further 2 minutes to heat through. Season to taste with salt and pepper.

Serve the risotto immediately, sprinkled with parsley.

ravioli with crabmeat & ricotta

makes 16 ravioli

ingredients
300 g/10½ oz type 00 pasta
   flour or strong white flour
1 tsp salt
3 eggs, beaten
70 g/2½ oz butter, melted

filling
175 g/6 oz white crabmeat
175 g/6 oz ricotta cheese
finely grated rind of 1 lemon
pinch of dried chilli flakes
2 tbsp chopped fresh
   flat-leaf parsley
salt and pepper

>**1** Sift the flour and salt onto a board or work surface, make a well in the centre and add the eggs.

>**2** Stir with a fork to gradually incorporate the flour into the liquid to form a dough.

>**3** Knead for about 5 minutes, until the dough is smooth. Wrap in clingfilm and leave to rest for 20 minutes.

>**4** For the filling, stir together the crabmeat, ricotta, lemon rind, chilli flakes and parsley. Season to taste with salt and pepper.

>5 Roll the dough with a pasta machine or by hand to a thickness of about 3 mm/⅛ inch and cut into 32 x 6-cm/2½-inch squares.

>6 Place a spoonful of the filling in the centre of half the squares.

>7 Brush the edges with water and place the remaining squares on top, pressing to seal.

>8 Bring a saucepan of lightly salted water to the boil. Add the ravioli, bring back to the boil and cook for 3 minutes, or until tender but still firm to the bite. Drain well.

Drizzle the melted butter over the ravioli, sprinkle with pepper and serve immediately.

vegetables & dairy

tomato soup

serves 4

ingredients
2 tbsp olive oil
1 large onion, chopped
400 g/14 oz canned peeled
  plum tomatoes
300 ml/10 fl oz chicken stock
  or vegetable stock
1 tbsp tomato purée
1 tsp hot chilli sauce
handful of fresh basil leaves
salt and pepper

>1 Heat the oil in a large saucepan over a medium heat, then add the onion and fry for 4–5 minutes, stirring, until soft.

>2 Add the tomatoes with their can juices, stock, tomato purée, chilli sauce and half the basil leaves.

Serve the soup in warmed serving bowls, garnished with the remaining basil leaves.

3 Purée with an electric hand-held blender until smooth, then transfer to the pan.

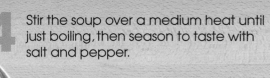**4** Stir the soup over a medium heat until just boiling, then season to taste with salt and pepper.

minestrone soup

serves 4

ingredients
2 tbsp olive oil
2 garlic cloves, chopped
2 red onions, chopped
75 g/2¾ oz Parma ham, sliced
1 red pepper, deseeded and
 chopped
1 orange pepper, deseeded
 and chopped
400 g/14 oz canned chopped
 tomatoes
1 litre/1¾ pints vegetable stock
1 celery stick, chopped
400 g/14 oz canned borlotti
 beans, drained
100 g/3½ oz green leafy
 cabbage, shredded
75 g/2¾ oz frozen peas
1 tbsp chopped fresh parsley
75 g/2¾ oz dried vermicelli
 pasta
salt and pepper
freshly grated Parmesan
 cheese, to serve

>1 Heat the oil in a large saucepan. Add the garlic, onions and ham and cook over a medium heat, stirring, for 3 minutes, until slightly softened.

>2 Add the red pepper and orange pepper and the chopped tomatoes and cook for a further 2 minutes, stirring. Stir in the stock, then add the celery.

Sprinkle with the Parmesan cheese and serve immediately.

> **>3** Add the beans to the pan with the cabbage, peas and parsley. Season to taste with salt and pepper. Bring to the boil, then reduce the heat and simmer for 30 minutes.

> **>4** Add the pasta to the pan. Cook for a further 8–10 minutes, or according to the packet instructions. Remove from the heat and ladle into bowls.

cheese & tomato pizza

makes 1 pizza

ingredients
pizza dough
225 g/8 oz plain flour,
   plus extra for dusting
1 tsp salt

1 tsp easy-blend dried yeast
1 tbsp olive oil, plus extra for
   oiling
6 tbsp lukewarm water

topping
6 tomatoes, thinly sliced
175 g/6 oz mozzarella
   cheese, drained and
   thinly sliced

2 tbsp shredded fresh basil
2 tbsp olive oil
salt and pepper

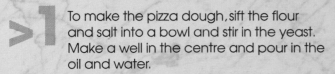

>1 To make the pizza dough, sift the flour and salt into a bowl and stir in the yeast. Make a well in the centre and pour in the oil and water.

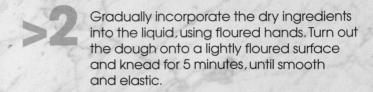

>2 Gradually incorporate the dry ingredients into the liquid, using floured hands. Turn out the dough onto a lightly floured surface and knead for 5 minutes, until smooth and elastic.

>3 Return the dough to a clean bowl, cover with lightly oiled clingfilm and leave to rise in a warm place for about 1 hour, or until doubled in size.

>4 Preheat the oven to 230°C/450°F/ Gas Mark 8. Lightly oil a baking sheet.

>5 Turn out the dough onto a lightly floured surface and knock back. Knead briefly, then roll out into a round about 5 mm/¼ inch thick.

>6 Transfer the pizza base to the prepared baking sheet and push up the edges with your fingers to form a small rim.

>7 For the topping, arrange the tomato and mozzarella slices over the pizza base.

>8 Season to taste with salt and pepper, sprinkle with the basil and drizzle with the oil. Bake in the preheated oven for 20–25 minutes, until golden brown.

Cut into slices and serve immediately.

goat's cheese tarts
makes about 12

ingredients

melted butter, for greasing
400 g/14 oz ready-rolled
  puff pastry

flour, for dusting
1 egg, beaten
about 3 tbsp onion relish or
  tomato relish

350 g/12 oz goat's cheese
  logs, sliced into rounds
olive oil, for drizzling
pepper

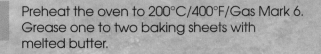

>1 Preheat the oven to 200°C/400°F/Gas Mark 6. Grease one to two baking sheets with melted butter.

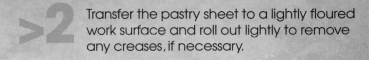

>2 Transfer the pastry sheet to a lightly floured work surface and roll out lightly to remove any creases, if necessary.

>3 Use a 7.5-cm/3-inch pastry cutter to stamp out as many rounds as possible.

>4 Place the rounds on the baking sheets and press gently about 2.5 cm/1 inch from the edge of each with a 5-cm/2-inch pastry cutter.

>5 Brush the rounds with the beaten egg and prick with a fork.

>6 Top each round with a teaspoon of the relish and a slice of the goat's cheese.

>7 Drizzle with oil and sprinkle over a little black pepper.

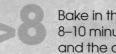

>8 Bake in the preheated oven for 8–10 minutes, or until the pastry is crisp and the cheese is bubbling.

Serve warm.

egg tortilla with feta & sweetcorn

serves 3–4

ingredients

350 g/12 oz potatoes
2 tbsp olive oil
1 onion, chopped
1 courgette, coarsely
  grated

200 g/7 oz canned
  sweetcorn, drained
6 eggs
100 g/3½ oz feta cheese
  (drained weight),
  crumbled

salt and pepper
paprika, to garnish

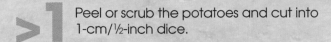 **>1** Peel or scrub the potatoes and cut into 1-cm/½-inch dice.

 >2 Cook the potatoes in a saucepan of lightly salted boiling water for 5 minutes, or until just tender. Drain.

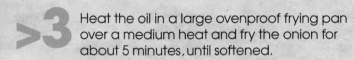 **>3** Heat the oil in a large ovenproof frying pan over a medium heat and fry the onion for about 5 minutes, until softened.

 >4 Stir in the courgette and potatoes, then cook for 2 minutes. Stir in the sweetcorn.

Beat the eggs lightly with salt and pepper to taste.

Stir the eggs into the pan, then scatter over the feta cheese. Cook for 4–6 minutes, until almost set.

>7

Meanwhile, preheat the grill to high. Place the tortilla under the preheated grill for 2–3 minutes, until set and golden brown.

>8

Sprinkle the tortilla with paprika and cut into four to six wedges.

Serve the tortilla hot or cold.

chilli bean stew

serves 4–6

ingredients

2 tbsp olive oil
1 onion, chopped
2–4 garlic cloves, chopped
2 fresh red chillies, deseeded
  and sliced
225 g/8 oz canned kidney
beans, drained and rinsed
225 g/8 oz canned cannellini
  beans, drained and rinsed
225 g/8 oz canned chickpeas,
  drained and rinsed
1 tbsp tomato purée
700–850 ml/1¼–1½ pints
vegetable stock
1 red pepper, deseeded and
  chopped
4 tomatoes, chopped
175 g/6 oz shelled fresh broad
  beans
1 tbsp chopped fresh
  coriander
paprika, to garnish
soured cream, to serve

>**1** Heat the oil in a large, heavy-based saucepan with a tight-fitting lid. Add the onion, garlic and chillies and cook, stirring frequently, for 5 minutes until soft.

>**2** Add the kidney beans, cannellini beans and chickpeas. Blend the tomato purée with a little of the stock and pour over the bean mixture, then add the remaining stock.

Garnish with the remaining chopped coriander and a pinch of paprika and serve topped with spoonfuls of soured cream.

>3 Bring to the boil, then reduce the heat and simmer for 10–15 minutes. Add the red pepper, tomatoes and broad beans.

>4 Simmer for a further 15–20 minutes or until all the vegetables are tender. Stir in most of the chopped coriander.

tacos with chickpea salsa

serves 4

ingredients

2 firm, ripe avocados
1 tbsp lime juice
1 tomato, diced
1 tbsp olive oil
1 small onion, sliced

400 g/14 oz canned
  chickpeas, drained
1 tsp mild chilli powder
8 Cos lettuce leaves
8 tacos

2 tbsp chopped fresh
  coriander, plus extra sprigs
  to garnish
salt and pepper
150 ml/5 fl oz soured cream,
  to serve

> **1** Halve, stone, peel and dice the avocados and toss with the lime juice.

> **2** Stir in the tomato and season well with salt and pepper.

> **3** Heat the oil in a saucepan and fry the onion for 3–4 minutes, or until golden brown.

> **4** Mash the chickpeas with a fork and stir into the pan with the chilli powder. Heat gently, stirring, for 2 minutes.

>5 Divide the lettuce between the tacos. Stir the chopped coriander into the avocado and tomato mixture, then spoon into the tacos.

>6 Add a spoonful of the chickpea mixture to each taco and top with a spoonful of soured cream.

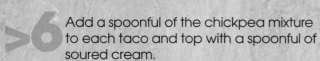

Garnish with corlander sprigs and serve immediately.

nut roast

serves 4

ingredients
2 tbsp olive oil, plus extra
 for brushing
1 large onion, finely
 chopped
100 g/3½ oz ground
 almonds
100 g/3½ oz cashew nuts,
 finely chopped
55 g/2 oz fresh wholemeal
 breadcrumbs
100 ml/3½ fl oz vegetable
 stock
finely grated rind and juice
 of 1 small lemon
1 tbsp finely chopped
 rosemary leaves
salt and pepper
fresh rosemary sprigs and
 lemon slices, to garnish

> **1** Preheat the oven to 200°C/400°F/Gas Mark 6.
Brush a 700-ml/1¼-pint loaf tin with oil and line
with baking paper.

> **2** Heat the oil in a large saucepan, add
the onion and fry over a medium heat,
stirring, for 3–4 minutes until soft.

> **1** Preheat the grill to high. Cut the polenta into eight slices and arrange on a baking sheet with the mushrooms.

> **2** Melt the butter in a small saucepan with the garlic. Stir in the parsley and chives.

> **3** Brush the mushrooms and polenta with the herb butter and season to taste with salt and pepper.

> **4** Cook under the preheated grill for 6–8 minutes, turning once, until the polenta is golden and mushrooms are tender.

> **>5** Bring a saucepan of water to just under boiling point. Break the eggs carefully into the water.

> **>6** Poach the eggs for about 3 minutes, until just set. Lift out with a slotted spoon.

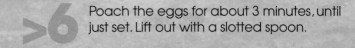

> **>7** Place two slices of polenta on each serving plate and add a small handful of spinach leaves.

> **>8** Top each with a mushroom, then add a poached egg and spoon over the remaining herb butter.

Garnish with chives and Parmesan cheese shavings and serve.

stroganoff

salt and pepper
fresh flat-leaf parsley sprigs,
  to garnish

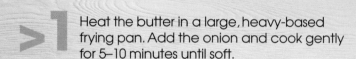

>1 Heat the butter in a large, heavy-based frying pan. Add the onion and cook gently for 5–10 minutes until soft.

>2 Add the mushrooms to the frying pan and stir-fry for a few minutes until they begin to soften.

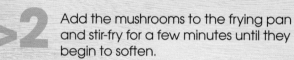

246

Garnish with extra paprika and parsley sprigs and serve immediately.

>3 Stir in the tomato purée and mustard, then add the crème fraîche. Cook gently, stirring constantly, for 5 minutes.

>4 Stir in the paprika and season to taste with salt and pepper.

mushroom & cauliflower cheese crumble

serves 4

ingredients

1 cauliflower, cut into florets
55 g/2 oz butter
115 g/4 oz button
  mushrooms, sliced
salt and pepper

topping

115 g/4 oz dry breadcrumbs
2 tbsp grated Parmesan
  cheese
1 tsp dried oregano
1 tsp dried parsley
25 g/1 oz butter

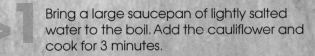

>1 Bring a large saucepan of lightly salted water to the boil. Add the cauliflower and cook for 3 minutes.

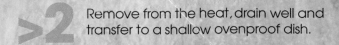

>2 Remove from the heat, drain well and transfer to a shallow ovenproof dish.

>3 Preheat the oven to 230°C/450°F/Gas Mark 8. Melt the butter in a small frying pan over a medium heat. Add the mushrooms, stir and cook gently for 3 minutes.

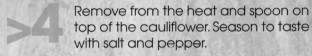

>4 Remove from the heat and spoon on top of the cauliflower. Season to taste with salt and pepper.

> **5** To make the topping, combine the breadcrumbs, Parmesan cheese and herbs in a small mixing bowl, then sprinkle over the vegetables.

> **6** Dice the butter and dot over the breadcrumb mixture. Bake in the preheated oven for 15 minutes, or until the topping is golden brown.

Serve straight from the cooking dish.

risotto with peas & gorgonzola

serves 4

ingredients

2 tbsp olive oil
25 g/1 oz butter
1 onion, finely chopped
1 garlic clove, finely
  chopped
350 g/12 oz risotto rice
150 ml/5 fl oz dry white wine
1.3 litres/2¼ pints vegetable
  stock
350 g/12 oz frozen peas
150 g/5½ oz Gorgonzola
  cheese, crumbled
2 tbsp chopped fresh mint
salt and pepper

>**1** Heat the oil and butter in a deep saucepan. Add the onion and cook, stirring frequently, for 3–4 minutes, until softened.

>**2** Add the garlic and rice and mix to coat in the butter and oil. Cook, stirring constantly, for 2–3 minutes, or until the grains are translucent. Add the wine and cook, stirring constantly, for 1 minute, until reduced.

Serve the risotto immediately.

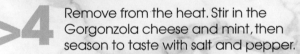

> **3** Gradually add the hot stock, a ladleful at a time. Cook, stirring, for 15 minutes, then stir in the peas and cook for a further 5 minutes, until the liquid is absorbed and the rice is creamy.

> **4** Remove from the heat. Stir in the Gorgonzola cheese and mint, then season to taste with salt and pepper.

cannelloni with spinach & ricotta

serves 4

ingredients
melted butter, for greasing
12 dried cannelloni tubes,
  each about 7.5 cm/
  3 inches long
salt and pepper

filling
140 g/5 oz frozen spinach,
  thawed and drained
115 g/4 oz ricotta cheese
1 egg

3 tbsp grated pecorino
  cheese
pinch of freshly grated
  nutmeg
salt and pepper

cheese sauce
25 g/1 oz butter
2 tbsp plain flour
600 ml/1 pint hot milk
85 g/3 oz Gruyère cheese,
  grated
salt and pepper

> **1** Preheat the oven to 180°C/350°F/Gas Mark 4. Grease a rectangular ovenproof dish with the melted butter.

> **2** Bring a large saucepan of lightly salted water to the boil. Add the cannelloni tubes, bring back to the boil and cook for 6–7 minutes, until nearly tender. Drain and rinse, then spread out on a clean tea towel.

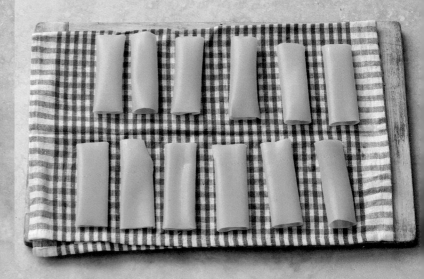

> **3** For the filling, put the spinach and ricotta into a food processor and process briefly until combined. Add the egg and pecorino cheese and process to a smooth paste. Transfer to a bowl, add the nutmeg and season to taste with salt and pepper.

> **4** Spoon the filling into a piping bag fitted with a 1-cm/½-inch nozzle. Carefully open a cannelloni tube and pipe in a little of the filling. Place the filled tube in the prepared dish and repeat.

>5 For the cheese sauce, melt the butter in a saucepan. Add the flour to the butter and cook over a low heat, stirring constantly, for 1 minute.

>6 Remove from the heat and gradually stir in the hot milk. Return to the heat and bring to the boil, stirring constantly. Simmer over a low heat, stirring frequently, for 10 minutes, until thickened and smooth.

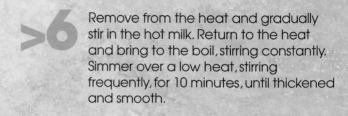

>7 Remove from the heat, stir in the Gruyère cheese and season to taste with salt and pepper.

>8 Spoon the cheese sauce over the filled cannelloni. Cover the dish with foil and bake in the preheated oven for 20–25 minutes.

Serve immediately.

pappardelle with cherry tomatoes & rocket

serves 4

ingredients
400 g/14 oz dried
  pappardelle
2 tbsp olive oil
1 garlic clove, chopped
350 g/12 oz cherry
  tomatoes, halved
85 g/3 oz rocket leaves
300 g/10½ oz mozzarella,
  chopped
salt and pepper
grated Parmesan cheese,
  to serve

> **1** Bring a large saucepan of lightly salted water to the boil. Add the pasta, bring back to the boil and cook for 8–10 minutes, or until tender but still firm to the bite.

> **2** Meanwhile, heat the oil in a frying pan over a medium heat and fry the garlic, stirring, for 1 minute, without browning.

Serve the pasta in wide dishes, sprinkled with Parmesan cheese.

>3 Add the tomatoes, season well with salt and pepper and cook gently for 2–3 minutes, until softened.

>4 Drain the pasta and stir into the frying pan. Add the rocket leaves and mozzarella, then stir until the leaves wilt.

macaroni cheese

serves 4

ingredients

250 g/9 oz dried macaroni
   pasta
600 ml/1 pint milk
½ tsp grated nutmeg

55 g/2 oz butter, plus extra
   for cooking the pasta
55 g/2 oz plain flour
200 g/7 oz Cheddar cheese,
   grated

55 g/2 oz freshly grated
   Parmesan cheese
salt and pepper

>1 Bring a large saucepan of lightly salted water to the boil. Add the pasta and cook for 8–10 minutes, or until tender but still firm to the bite. Remove from the heat and drain. Add a small knob of butter, return to the saucepan and cover to keep warm.

>2 Put the milk and nutmeg into a saucepan over a low heat and heat until warm, but do not bring to the boil.

>3 Melt the butter in a heavy-based saucepan over a low heat, then add the flour and stir to make a roux. Cook gently for 2 minutes.

>4 Add the milk a little at a time, whisking it into the roux, then cook for about 10–15 minutes to make a loose, custard-style sauce.

>5 Add three quarters of the Cheddar cheese and Parmesan cheese and stir through until they have melted in. Season to taste with salt and pepper and remove from the heat.

>6 Preheat the grill to high. Put the macaroni into a shallow heatproof dish, then pour the sauce over.

>7 Scatter the remaining cheese over the top and place the dish under the preheated grill.

>8 Grill until the cheese begins to brown.

Serve immediately.

pasta all' arrabbiata

serves 4

ingredients
150 ml/5 fl oz dry white wine
1 tbsp sun-dried tomato
  purée
2 fresh red chillies
2 garlic cloves, finely
  chopped
4 tbsp chopped fresh
  flat-leaf parsley
400 g/14 oz dried penne
salt and pepper
fresh pecorino cheese
  shavings, to garnish

sugocasa
5 tbsp extra virgin olive oil
450 g/1 lb plum tomatoes,
  chopped
salt and pepper

1 To make the sugocasa, heat the oil in a frying pan over a high heat until almost smoking. Add the tomatoes and cook, stirring frequently, for 2–3 minutes.

>2 Reduce the heat to low and cook for about 20 minutes. Season to taste with salt and pepper. Using a wooden spoon, press through a non-metallic sieve into a saucepan.

Sprinkle with the remaining parsley, garnish with cheese shavings and serve immediately.

>3 Add the wine, tomato purée, whole chillies and garlic to the pan and bring to the boil. Reduce the heat and simmer gently, then remove the chillies. Check and adjust the seasoning, adding the chillies back in for a hotter sauce, then stir in half the parsley.

>4 Meanwhile, bring a large saucepan of lightly salted water to the boil. Add the pasta, bring back to the boil and cook for 8–10 minutes, or until tender but still firm to the bite. Add the sauce to the pasta and toss to coat.

aubergine gratin

serves 2

ingredients

4 tbsp olive oil
2 onions, finely chopped
2 garlic cloves, very finely
  chopped
2 aubergines, thickly sliced

3 tbsp chopped fresh
  flat-leaf parsley, plus extra
  sprigs to garnish
½ tsp dried thyme

400 g/14 oz canned
  chopped tomatoes
175 g/6 oz mozzarella
  cheese, coarsely grated

6 tbsp freshly grated
  Parmesan cheese
salt and pepper

>1 Heat the oil in a flameproof casserole over a medium heat. Add the onions and cook for 5 minutes, or until soft.

>2 Add the garlic and cook for a few seconds, or until just beginning to colour. Using a slotted spoon, transfer the onion mixture to a plate.

>3 Add the aubergine slices to the casserole in batches and cook until lightly browned. Transfer to another plate.

>4 Preheat the oven to 200°C/400°F/ Gas Mark 6. Arrange a layer of aubergine slices in the base of the casserole or a shallow ovenproof dish.

>5 Sprinkle with some of the parsley, thyme, and salt and pepper to taste.

 >6 Add layers of onion, tomatoes and mozzarella cheese, sprinkling parsley, thyme, and salt and pepper to taste over each layer.

>7 Continue layering, finishing with a layer of aubergine slices.

>8 Sprinkle with the Parmesan cheese and bake, uncovered, in the preheated oven for 20–30 minutes, or until the top is golden and the aubergines are tender.

Serve hot, garnished with parsley sprigs.

tomato ratatouille

serves 4

ingredients
1 tsp olive oil
1 onion, cut into small
   wedges
2–4 garlic cloves, chopped
1 small aubergine, chopped
1 red pepper, deseeded
   and chopped
1 yellow pepper, deseeded
   and chopped
1 courgette, chopped
2 tbsp tomato purée
115 g/4 oz mushrooms,
   halved
225 g/8 oz tomatoes,
   chopped
pepper
1 tbsp shredded fresh basil,
   to garnish
2 tbsp grated Parmesan
   cheese, to serve

>1 Heat the oil in a heavy-based saucepan.
Add the onion, garlic and aubergine and
cook, stirring frequently, for 3 minutes.

>2 Add the red and yellow peppers and
the courgette.

Divide the ratatouille between warmed dishes, garnish with shredded basil and serve with Parmesan cheese.

>3 Mix together the tomato purée and 3 tablespoons of water in a small bowl and stir into the pan. Bring to the boil, cover, reduce the heat to a simmer and cook for 10 minutes.

>4 Add the mushrooms and tomatoes, with pepper to taste, and continue to simmer for 12–15 minutes, stirring occasionally, until the vegetables are tender.

tofu stir-fry

serves 4

ingredients

2 tbsp sunflower oil

350 g/12 oz firm tofu, cubed

225 g/8 oz pak choi, roughly chopped

1 garlic clove, chopped

4 tbsp sweet chilli sauce

2 tbsp light soy sauce

Transfer to individual dishes and serve immediately.

jamaican rice & peas with tofu

serves 4

ingredients

250 g/9 oz firm tofu
2 tbsp chopped fresh
 thyme, plus extra sprigs to
 garnish

2 tbsp olive oil
1 onion, sliced
1 garlic clove, crushed
1 small fresh red chilli,
 chopped

400 ml/14 fl oz vegetable
 stock
200 g/7 oz basmati rice
4 tbsp coconut cream

400 g/14 oz canned red
 kidney beans, drained
salt and pepper

Cut the tofu into bite-sized cubes. Toss with half the chopped thyme and sprinkle with salt and pepper to taste.

Heat 1 tablespoon of the oil in a frying pan and fry the tofu, stirring occasionally, for 2 minutes. Remove and keep warm.

>**3** Fry the onion in the remaining oil, stirring, for 3–4 minutes.

>**4** Stir in the garlic, chilli and the remaining chopped thyme, then add the stock and bring to the boil.

5 Stir in the rice, then reduce the heat, cover and simmer for 12–15 minutes, until the rice is tender.

6 Stir in the coconut cream and beans, season to taste with salt and pepper and cook gently for 2–3 minutes.

Spoon the tofu over the rice and serve hot, garnished with thyme sprigs.

desserts

tiramisù

serves 6

ingredients

4 egg yolks

100 g/3½ oz caster sugar

1 tsp vanilla extract

500 g/1 lb 2 oz mascarpone
cheese

2 egg whites

175 ml/6 fl oz strong black
coffee

125 ml/4 fl oz rum or brandy

24 sponge fingers

2 tbsp cocoa powder

2 tbsp finely grated plain
chocolate

>**1** Whisk the egg yolks with the sugar and vanilla extract in a heatproof bowl set over a saucepan of barely simmering water.

>**2** When the mixture is pale and the whisk leaves a ribbon trail when lifted, remove the bowl from the heat and set aside to cool. Whisk occasionally to prevent a skin from forming.

>**3** When the egg yolk mixture is cool, whisk in the mascarpone cheese until thoroughly combined.

>**4** Whisk the egg whites in a separate, spotlessly clean bowl until they form soft peaks, then gently fold them into the mascarpone mixture.

Combine the coffee and rum in a shallow dish. Briefly dip eight of the sponge fingers in the mixture, then arrange in the base of a serving dish.

>6 Spoon one third of the mascarpone mixture on top, spreading it out evenly. Repeat the layers twice, finishing with the mascarpone mixture. Chill for at least 1 hour.

To serve, sift the cocoa evenly over the top
and sprinkle with the chocolate.

mini apple crumbles

serves 4

ingredients
2 large Bramley apples, peeled, cored and chopped
3 tbsp maple syrup
juice of ½ lemon
½ tsp ground allspice
55 g/2 oz unsalted butter
100 g/3½ oz porridge oats
40 g/1½ oz light muscovado sugar

> **1** Preheat the oven to 220°C/425°F/Gas Mark 7. Place a baking sheet in the oven to heat. Put the apples into a saucepan and stir in the maple syrup, lemon juice and allspice.

> **2** Bring to the boil over a high heat, then reduce the heat to medium, cover the pan and cook for 5 minutes, or until almost tender.

Serve the crumbles warm.

>3 Meanwhile, melt the butter in a separate saucepan, then remove from the heat and stir in the oats and sugar.

>4 Divide the apples between four 200-ml/7-fl oz ovenproof dishes. Sprinkle over the oat mixture. Place on the baking sheet in the preheated oven and bake for 10 minutes, until lightly browned and bubbling.

strawberry cheesecake

serves 8

ingredients
base
55 g/2 oz unsalted butter
200 g/7 oz digestive biscuits,
  crushed
85 g/3 oz chopped walnuts

filling
450 g/1 lb mascarpone
  cheese
2 eggs, beaten
3 tbsp caster sugar

250 g/9 oz white chocolate,
  broken into pieces
300 g/10½ oz strawberries,
  hulled and quartered

topping
175 g/6 oz mascarpone
  cheese
50 g/1¾ oz white chocolate
  shavings
4 strawberries, halved

288

>**1** Preheat the oven to 150°C/300°F/Gas Mark 2. Melt the butter in a saucepan over a low heat and stir in the crushed biscuits and walnuts.

>**2** Spoon into a 23-cm/9-inch springform cake tin and press evenly over the base with the back of a spoon. Set aside.

>**3** To make the filling, beat the mascarpone cheese in a bowl until smooth, then beat in the eggs and sugar.

>**4** Melt the white chocolate in a heatproof bowl set over a saucepan of gently simmering water, stirring until smooth. Remove from the heat and leave to cool slightly, then stir into the cheese mixture. Stir in the strawberries.

>5 Spoon the mixture into the cake tin, spread evenly and smooth the surface. Bake in the preheated oven for 1 hour, or until just firm.

>6 Turn off the oven and leave the cheesecake inside with the door slightly ajar until completely cold. Transfer to a serving plate.

For the topping, spread the mascarpone cheese on top, decorate with the chocolate shavings and the strawberry halves and serve.

lemon meringue pie

serves 6–8

ingredients

pastry

150 g/5½ oz plain flour,
  plus extra for dusting
85 g/3 oz butter, cut into
  small pieces, plus extra for
  greasing

35 g/1¼ oz icing sugar, sifted
finely grated rind of
  ½ lemon
½ egg yolk, beaten
1½ tbsp milk

filling

3 tbsp cornflour
300 ml/10 fl oz water
juice and grated rind of
  2 lemons
175 g/6 oz caster sugar
2 eggs, separated

> **1** To make the pastry, sift the flour into a bowl. Rub in the butter with your fingertips until the mixture resembles fine breadcrumbs.

> **2** Mix in the remaining pastry Ingredients. Turn out onto a lightly floured work surface and knead briefly. Wrap in clingfilm and chill in the refrigerator for 30 minutes.

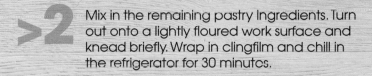

> **3** Preheat the oven to 180°C/350°F/Gas Mark 4. Grease a 20-cm/8-inch round tart tin. Roll out the pastry to a thickness of 5 mm/¼ inch, then use to line the tin.

> **4** Prick all over with a fork, line with baking paper and fill with baking beans. Bake blind in the preheated oven for 15 minutes.

>5 Remove the pastry case from the oven and take out the paper and beans. Reduce the oven temperature to 150°C/300°F/Gas Mark 2.

>6 To make the filling, mix the cornflour with a little of the water to form a paste. Put the remaining water in a saucepan. Stir in the lemon juice, lemon rind and cornflour paste.

>7 Bring to the boil, stirring. Cook for 2 minutes. Leave to cool slightly. Stir in 5 tablespoons of the caster sugar and the egg yolks. Pour into the pastry case.

>8 Whisk the egg whites until stiff. Gradually whisk in the remaining caster sugar and spread over the pie. Return to the oven and bake for a further 40 minutes.

Remove from the oven, leave to cool and serve.

chocolate mousse

serves 4–6

ingredients

225 g/8 oz plain chocolate,
   chopped
2 tbsp brandy, Grand
   Marnier or Cointreau
4 tbsp water
30 g/1 oz unsalted butter,
   diced
3 large eggs, separated
¼ tsp cream of tartar
55 g/2 oz sugar
125 ml/4 fl oz double cream

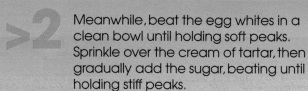

>1 Put the chocolate, brandy and water in a heatproof bowl set over a small saucepan over a low heat and stir until smooth. Remove from the heat. Beat in the butter and then the egg yolks, one at a time, until blended. Cool slightly.

>2 Meanwhile, beat the egg whites in a clean bowl until holding soft peaks. Sprinkle over the cream of tartar, then gradually add the sugar, beating until holding stiff peaks.

Spoon the mousse into individual bowls. Cover with clingfilm and chill for at least 3 hours before serving.

>3 Beat several tablespoons of the beaten egg white into the chocolate mixture to loosen.

>4 Whip the cream until holding soft peaks. Spoon the cream over the chocolate mixture, then add the remaining egg whites mixture. Use a spatula to fold the chocolate into the cream and egg whites mixture.

panna cotta with spiced plums

serves 4

ingredients

panna cotta
4 leaves gelatine
300 ml/10 fl oz milk
250 g/9 oz mascarpone
  cheese

100 g/3½ oz caster sugar
1 vanilla pod, halved
  lengthways

spiced plums
8 red plums, halved and
  stoned
3 tbsp clear honey
1 cinnamon stick

thinly pared strip of orange
  zest
1 tbsp balsamic vinegar

> **1** Soak the gelatine leaves in 4 tablespoons of the milk for 10 minutes.

> **2** Place the remaining milk, the mascarpone cheese, sugar and vanilla pod in a saucepan and heat gently, stirring until smooth, then bring to the boil.

> **3** Remove from the heat, discard the vanilla pod and add the gelatine mixture, stirring until completely dissolved.

> **4** Pour into 4 x 200-ml/7-fl oz individual pudding moulds. Leave to chill in the refrigerator until set.

299

>5 Place the plums, honey, cinnamon stick, orange zest and vinegar in a saucepan. Cover and cook gently for 10 minutes, or until the plums are tender.

>6 Dip the base of each mould quickly in hot water and turn out onto a serving plate.

Serve the panna cotta with the spiced plums
on the side.

stuffed peaches with amaretto

serves 4

ingredients
55 g/2 oz unsalted butter
4 peaches
2 tbsp soft light brown sugar
55 g/2 oz amaretti biscuits,
  crushed
2 tbsp amaretto
125 ml/4 fl oz single cream,
  to serve

>1 Preheat the oven to 180°C/350°F/Gas Mark 4. Grease a baking dish, large enough to hold eight peach halves in a single layer, with 15 g/½ oz of the butter.

>2 Halve the peaches and remove and discard the stones.

Pour over the amaretto and serve hot with cream.

> 3 Beat together the remaining butter and the sugar in a bowl until creamy. Add the biscuit crumbs and mix well.

> 4 Arrange the peach halves, cut-side up, in the prepared baking dish and fill the cavities with the biscuit mixture. Bake in the preheated oven for 20–25 minutes, or until tender.

pineapple dessert
serves 6

ingredients

1 pineapple
4 tbsp sultanas
2 tbsp raisins
4 tbsp maple syrup
4 tbsp white rum

1 egg yolk
1 tbsp cornflour
½ tsp vanilla extract
¼ tsp ground ginger
2 egg whites
2 tbsp muscovado sugar

>1 Preheat the oven to 240°C/475°F/Gas Mark 9. Cut off the leafy top and the base of the pineapple and discard.

>2 Stand the pineapple upright and slice off the skin. Remove any remaining 'eyes' with the tip of a small sharp knife. Cut in half lengthways and remove the hard woody core, then slice the flesh.

>3 Arrange the pineapple slices in a large ovenproof dish and sprinkle over the sultanas and raisins. Drizzle with half the maple syrup and half the rum. Bake in the preheated oven for 5 minutes.

>4 Meanwhile, mix the remaining maple syrup and rum with the egg yolk, cornflour, vanilla extract and ginger in a bowl.

> **5** Whip the egg whites in a separate bowl until soft peaks form. Stir 2 tablespoons of the egg white into the egg yolk mixture, then fold the remaining egg yolk mixture into the egg whites.

> **6** Spread the topping over the hot pineapple, sprinkle the sugar over the top and bake in the preheated oven for 5 minutes, or until golden brown.

Serve immediately.

coconut pancakes with pineapple

serves 4

ingredients
140 g/5 oz plain flour
2 tbsp caster sugar
2 eggs

400 ml/14 fl oz coconut milk
1 medium pineapple
groundnut oil, for frying

toasted coconut, to
  decorate
canned coconut cream,
  to serve

> **1** Sift the flour and sugar into a bowl and make a well in the centre.

> **2** Add the eggs and coconut milk to the well and stir into the flour, then whisk to a smooth, bubbly batter.

> **3** Stand the pineapple upright and slice off the skin. Remove any remaining 'eyes' with the tip of a small knife. Cut in half lengthways and remove the hard woody core. Cut the flesh into chunks.

> **4** Heat a small amount of oil in a heavy-based frying pan and pour in a little batter, swirling to cover the pan.

> **5** Cook the pancake on a high heat until set and golden underneath.

> **6** Toss or turn the pancake and cook until golden on the other side.

> **7** Repeat with the remaining batter to make 8–10 pancakes, stacking alternately with non-stick paper between whilst making the rest.

> **8** Fill the pancakes with pieces of pineapple and fold into fan shapes to serve.

Sprinkle the pancakes with toasted shreds of coconut and serve drizzled with coconut cream.

raspberry croissant puddings

serves 4

ingredients

30 g/1 oz unsalted butter,
  melted
4 croissants

225 g/8 oz fresh raspberries
4 tbsp maple syrup
350 ml/12 fl oz milk

2 large eggs, beaten
1 tsp vanilla extract
freshly grated nutmeg,
  for sprinkling

> **>1** Preheat the oven to 220°C/425°F/ Gas Mark 7. Place a baking sheet on the middle shelf.

> **>2** Brush four 350-ml/12-fl oz ovenproof dishes with half the butter.

> **>3** Chop the croissants into bite-sized chunks. Mix with the raspberries and divide between the dishes.

> **>4** Spoon 1 tablespoon of the maple syrup over the contents of each dish.

Heat the milk until almost boiling, then quickly beat in the eggs and vanilla extract.

Pour the milk mixture evenly over the dishes, pressing the croissants down lightly.

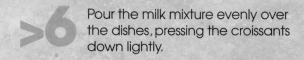

Drizzle with the remaining butter and sprinkle a little nutmeg over each dish.

Place the dishes on the baking tray and bake in the preheated oven for about 20 minutes, until lightly set.

Serve hot.

ricotta tart with chocolate & walnuts

serves 6

ingredients

115 g/4 oz caster sugar
125 g/4½ oz unsalted butter,
  softened
2 egg yolks
finely grated rind of 1 lemon
250 g/9 oz plain flour

filling

125 g/4½ oz plain
  chocolate, broken into
  pieces
250 g/9 oz ricotta cheese
40 g/1½ oz icing sugar,
  plus extra for dusting

2 tbsp dark rum
1 tsp vanilla extract
100 g/3½ oz walnuts,
  finely chopped

316

>1 Preheat the oven to 180°C/350°F/Gas Mark 4. Place the caster sugar, butter, egg yolks and lemon rind in a bowl and beat well to mix evenly.

>2 Add the flour and work the mixture with your fingers to make a smooth dough.

>3 Wrap the dough in clingfilm and leave to rest at room temperature for about 10 minutes.

>4 Melt the chocolate in a heatproof bowl set over a saucepan of hot water.

>5 Mix together the ricotta cheese, icing sugar, rum, vanilla extract and walnuts. Stir in the melted chocolate, mixing evenly.

>6 Roll out two thirds of the dough and press into the base and sides of a 23-cm/9-inch loose-based flan tin.

>7 Spoon the ricotta mixture into the pastry case, smoothing level.

>8 Roll out the remaining dough, cut into strips and arrange over the tart to form a lattice. Place on a baking sheet and bake in the preheated oven for 35–40 minutes, until firm and golden.

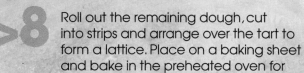

Serve the tart warm, dusted with
icing sugar.

fig tartlets
serves 4

ingredients

250 g/9 oz ready-made
 puff pastry
plain flour, for dusting

8 fresh ripe figs
1 tbsp caster sugar
½ tsp ground cinnamon

milk, for brushing
vanilla ice cream, to serve

>1 Preheat the oven to 190°C/375°F/Gas Mark 5. Roll out the pastry on a lightly floured surface to a thickness of 5 mm/¼ inch.

>2 Using a saucer as a guide, cut out 4 x 15-cm/6-inch rounds and place on a baking tray.

>3 Use a sharp knife to score a line halfway through each pastry round, about 1 cm/½ inch from the outer edge. Prick the centre all over with a fork.

>4 Slice the figs into quarters and arrange eight quarters over the centre of each pastry round.

>5 Mix together the sugar and cinnamon and sprinkle over the figs.

>6 Brush the edges of the pastry with milk and bake in the preheated oven for 15–20 minutes, until risen and golden brown.

Serve the tartlets warm with ice cream.

coconut ice cream

serves 4

ingredients
400 ml/14 fl oz coconut milk
140 g/5 oz caster sugar
150 ml/5 fl oz single cream
rind of ½ lime, finely grated
2 tbsp lime juice
curls of lime zest,
  to decorate

>1 Place half the coconut milk and the sugar in a saucepan and stir over a medium heat until the sugar has dissolved.

>2 Remove from the heat and stir in the remaining coconut milk, cream, lime rind and juice. Leave to cool completely.

Top with curled shreds of lime zest and serve.

>3 Transfer to a freezerproof container and freeze for 2 hours, whisking at hourly intervals.

>4 Serve the ice cream scooped into glasses or bowls.

butterscotch, mango & ginger sundaes

serves 4

ingredients

100 g/3½ oz light
   muscovado sugar
100 g/3½ oz golden syrup
55 g/2 oz unsalted butter

100 ml/3½ fl oz double
   cream
½ tsp vanilla extract
1 large, ripe mango
115 g/4 oz ginger biscuits

1 litre/1¾ pints vanilla ice
   cream
2 tbsp roughly chopped
   almonds, toasted

>1 To make the butterscotch sauce, melt the sugar, golden syrup and butter in a small pan and simmer for 3 minutes, stirring, until smooth.

>2 Stir in the cream and vanilla extract, then remove from the heat.

>3 Peel and stone the mango and cut into 1-cm/½-inch cubes.

>4 Place the ginger biscuits in a polythene bag and crush lightly with a rolling pin.

5 Place half the mango in four sundae glasses and top each with a scoop of the ice cream.

 6 Spoon over a little butterscotch sauce and sprinkle with crushed biscuits. Repeat with the remaining glasses.

Sprinkle some of the almonds over the top of
each sundae and serve immediately.

zabaglione

serves 4

ingredients
4 egg yolks
60 g/2¼ oz caster sugar
5 tbsp Marsala
amaretti biscuits, to serve

>1 Whisk the egg yolks with the sugar in a
heatproof bowl for about 1 minute.

>2 Gently whisk in the Marsala.

Serve with amaretti biscuits.

> **>3** Set the bowl over a saucepan of barely simmering water and whisk vigorously for 10–15 minutes, until thick, creamy and foamy.

> **>4** Immediately pour into serving glasses.

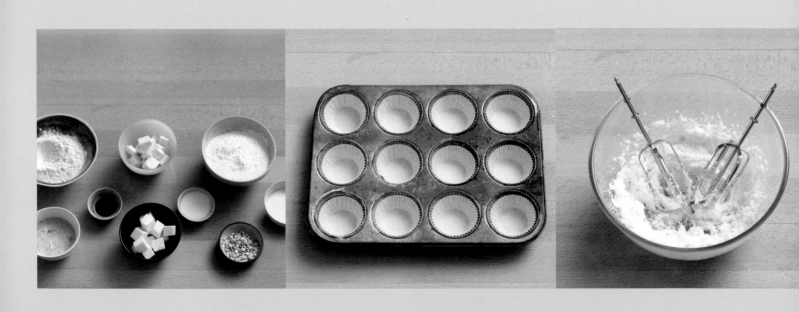

baking

chocolate cake

serves 8

ingredients

150 g/5½ oz plain white flour
25 g/1 oz cocoa powder
175 g/6 oz golden caster
  sugar
1 tbsp baking powder

175 g/6 oz unsalted butter,
  at room temperature, plus
  extra for greasing
3 eggs, beaten
1 tsp vanilla extract
2 tbsp milk

frosting

115 g/4 oz unsalted butter,
  at room temperature
200 g/7 oz icing sugar
2 tbsp cocoa powder
1 tsp vanilla extract

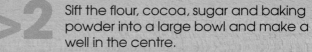
>**1** Preheat the oven to 180°C/350°F/Gas Mark 4. Grease and line the base and sides of two 20-cm/8-inch sandwich cake tins.

>**2** Sift the flour, cocoa, sugar and baking powder into a large bowl and make a well in the centre.

>**3** Beat the butter until soft. Add to the dry ingredients with the eggs, vanilla extract and milk. Beat lightly with a wooden spoon until just smooth.

>**4** Spoon the mixture into the prepared tins, smoothing with a palette knife. Bake in the preheated oven for 25–30 minutes, until risen and firm.

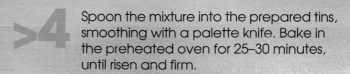

>5 Leave the cakes to cool in the tins for 2–3 minutes, then turn out onto a wire rack and leave to cool completely.

>6 To make the frosting, beat the butter until smooth and fluffy. Sift the icing sugar with the cocoa and beat into the butter until smooth.

>7 Stir in the vanilla extract with enough hot water to mix to a soft spreading consistency.

>8 When the cakes are cold, sandwich them together with half the frosting, then spread the remainder over the top, swirling with a palette knife.

Cut into slices and serve.

classic cherry cake

serves 8

ingredients

250 g/9 oz glacé cherries,
quartered
85 g/3 oz ground almonds
200 g/7 oz plain flour

1 tsp baking powder
200 g/7 oz unsalted butter,
plus extra for greasing
200 g/7 oz caster sugar

3 large eggs
finely grated rind and juice
of 1 lemon
6 sugar cubes, crushed

>1 Preheat the oven to 180°C/350°F/ Gas Mark 4. Grease and line a 20-cm/8-inch round cake tin.

>2 Stir together the cherries, almonds and 1 tablespoon of the flour. Sift the remaining flour into a separate bowl with the baking powder.

>3 Cream together the butter and sugar until light and fluffy. Gradually add the eggs, beating hard, until evenly mixed.

>4 Add the flour mixture and fold lightly and evenly into the creamed mixture with a metal spoon. Add the cherry mixture. Fold in evenly, then fold in the lemon rind and juice.

>5 Spoon the mixture into the prepared tin and sprinkle with the crushed sugar cubes. Bake in the preheated oven for 1–1¼ hours, or until risen and golden brown and shrinking from the sides of the tin.

>6 Leave to cool in the tin for about 15 minutes, then turn out onto a wire rack to cool completely.

Cut into slices and serve as
a mid-morning treat.

pineapple & coconut ring cake

serves 12

ingredients

425 g/15½ oz canned
  pineapple rings, drained
115 g/4 oz unsalted butter,
  softened, plus extra for
  greasing

175 g/6 oz caster sugar
2 eggs and 1 egg yolk,
  beaten together
225 g/8 oz plain flour
1 tsp baking powder

½ tsp bicarbonate of soda
40 g/1½ oz desiccated
  coconut

frosting

175 g/6 oz cream cheese
175 g/6 oz icing sugar

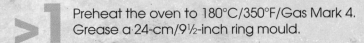

> **1** Preheat the oven to 180°C/350°F/Gas Mark 4. Grease a 24-cm/9½-inch ring mould.

> **2** Place the pineapple rings in a blender or food processor and process briefly until just crushed.

> **3** Beat together the butter and caster sugar until light and fluffy.

> **4** Gradually beat in the eggs until combined.

343

>5 Sift together the flour, baking powder and bicarbonate of soda over the egg mixture and fold in. Fold in the crushed pineapple and the coconut.

>6 Spoon the mixture into the prepared tin and bake in the preheated oven for 25 minutes until a skewer inserted into the centre comes out clean.

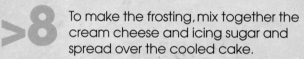

>7 Leave to cool in the tin for 10 minutes before turning out onto a wire rack to cool completely.

>8 To make the frosting, mix together the cream cheese and icing sugar and spread over the cooled cake.

Cut into slices and serve immediately.

banana coconut loaf cake

makes 1 loaf

ingredients

250 g/9 oz plain flour
1½ tsp baking powder
200 g/7 oz caster sugar
55 g/2 oz desiccated
  coconut

2 eggs
90 ml/6 tbsp sunflower oil,
  plus extra for greasing
2 ripe bananas, mashed
125 ml/4 fl oz soured cream

1 tsp vanilla extract
long shred coconut,
  toasted, to decorate

Preheat the oven to 180°C/350°F/Gas Mark 4. Grease and line a 1-litre/1¾ pint loaf tin.

Sift together the flour and baking powder in a large bowl.

>3 Stir in the sugar and coconut.

>4 Beat together the eggs, oil, bananas, cream and vanilla extract in a large bowl.

Stir into the dry ingredients, mixing until evenly combined.

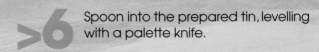

Spoon into the prepared tin, levelling with a palette knife.

>7 Bake in the preheated oven for about 1 hour or until risen, firm and golden brown.

>8 Cool in the tin for 15 minutes, then turn out onto a wire rack to cool completely.

Decorate with shreds of coconut and serve.

vanilla-frosted cupcakes

makes 12 cupcakes

ingredients
115 g/4 oz butter, softened
115 g/4 oz caster sugar
2 eggs, lightly beaten

115 g/4 oz self-raising flour
1 tbsp milk
1 tbsp coloured sprinkles

frosting
175 g/6 oz unsalted butter,
 softened
1 tsp vanilla extract
280 g/10 oz icing sugar,
 sifted

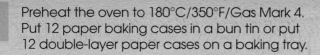 Preheat the oven to 180°C/350°F/Gas Mark 4. Put 12 paper baking cases in a bun tin or put 12 double-layer paper cases on a baking tray.

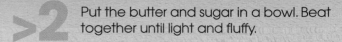 Put the butter and sugar in a bowl. Beat together until light and fluffy.

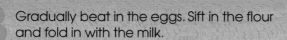 Gradually beat in the eggs. Sift in the flour and fold in with the milk.

>4 Spoon the mixture into the paper cases. Bake in the preheated oven for 20 minutes until golden brown and firm to the touch. Transfer to a wire rack to cool.

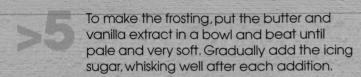

>5 To make the frosting, put the butter and vanilla extract in a bowl and beat until pale and very soft. Gradually add the icing sugar, whisking well after each addition.

>6 Spoon the frosting into a large piping bag fitted with a medium star-shaped nozzle and pipe swirls of frosting on the top of each cupcake.

Serve decorated with sprinkles.

chocolate butterfly cupcakes

makes 12 cupcakes

ingredients

125 g/4½ oz margarine, softened
125 g/4½ oz caster sugar
150 g/5½ oz self-raising flour, sifted

2 large eggs
2 tbsp cocoa powder
25 g/1 oz plain chocolate, melted

lemon buttercream

100 g/3½ oz unsalted butter, softened
225 g/8 oz icing sugar, sifted, plus extra for dusting

grated rind of ½ lemon
1 tbsp lemon juice

> **1** Preheat the oven to 180°C/350°F/Gas Mark 4. Place 12 paper cases in a shallow bun tin.

> **2** Place the margarine, caster sugar, flour, eggs and cocoa powder in a large bowl, and beat until the mixture is just smooth. Beat in the melted chocolate.

> **3** Spoon the mixture into the paper cases, filling them three-quarters full.

> **4** Bake in the preheated oven for 15 minutes, or until well risen. Remove from the oven and place on a wire rack to cool.

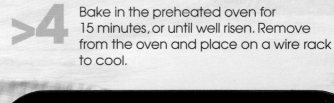

>**5** To make the buttercream, place the butter in a mixing bowl and beat until fluffy. Gradually add in the icing sugar, lemon rind and lemon juice, beating well with each addition.

>**6** Cut the top off each cake, using a serrated knife. Cut each cake top in half. Spread the lemon buttercream over the cut surface of each cake and push the two pieces of cake top into the icing to form wings.

Dust with icing sugar and serve.

low-fat blueberry muffins

makes 12 muffins

ingredients

225 g/8 oz plain flour
1 tsp bicarbonate of soda
¼ tsp salt
1 tsp ground allspice

115 g/4 oz caster sugar
3 large egg whites
3 tbsp low-fat margarine

150 ml/5 fl oz thick low-
   fat natural yogurt or
   blueberry-flavoured yogurt
1 tsp vanilla extract
85 g/3 oz fresh blueberries

> **1** Preheat the oven to 190°C/375°F/Gas Mark 5. Place 12 paper cases in a shallow bun tin.

> **2** Sift the flour, bicarbonate of soda, salt and half the allspice into a large mixing bowl. Add six tablespoons of the sugar and mix together well.

> **3** In a separate bowl whisk together the egg whites. Add the margarine, yogurt and vanilla extract and mix together well, then stir in the blueberries until thoroughly mixed.

> **4** Add the fruit mixture to the dry ingredients, then gently stir until just combined. Do not overstir – it is fine for it to be a little lumpy.

359

>5 Divide the mixture evenly between the paper cases to about two-thirds full. Mix the remaining sugar with the remaining allspice and sprinkle over the muffins.

>6 Bake in the preheated oven for 25 minutes, or until well risen. Remove the muffins from the oven.

Leave to cool or serve warm.

apricot, macadamia & white chocolate chunk muffins

makes 12 muffins

ingredients

280 g/10 oz plain flour
1 tbsp baking powder
115 g/ 4 oz golden caster sugar
85 g/3 oz ready to eat dried apricots, chopped
55 g/2 oz macadamia nuts, chopped
55 g/2 oz white chocolate, chopped
2 eggs, beaten
200 ml/7 fl oz buttermilk
100 ml/3½ fl oz sunflower oil

> **1** Preheat the oven to 200°C/400°F/Gas Mark 6. Place 12 paper muffin cases in a muffin tray or on a baking sheet.

> **2** Sift the flour and baking powder into a bowl and stir in the sugar, apricots, nuts and chocolate.

Serve the muffins warm, preferably on the day of making.

>3 Beat together the eggs, buttermilk and oil, then add to the bowl and stir to mix evenly.

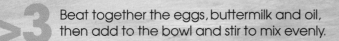

>4 Spoon the mixture into the muffin cases and bake in the preheated oven for 20–25 minutes, until well risen.

rocky road bars

makes 8 bars

ingredients

175 g/6 oz milk or plain
  chocolate
55 g/2 oz butter
100 g/3½ oz shortcake
  biscuits, broken into pieces

85 g/3 oz white mini
  marshmallows
85 g/3 oz walnuts or
  peanuts
icing sugar, sifted, for dusting

Line an 18-cm/7-inch square cake tin with baking paper.

Break the chocolate into squares and place in a heatproof bowl.

Set the bowl over a saucepan of gently simmering water and heat until the chocolate is melted, taking care that the bowl does not touch the water.

Add the butter and stir until melted and combined. Leave to cool slightly.

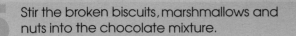

>5 Stir the broken biscuits, marshmallows and nuts into the chocolate mixture.

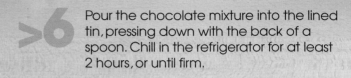

>6 Pour the chocolate mixture into the lined tin, pressing down with the back of a spoon. Chill in the refrigerator for at least 2 hours, or until firm.

>7 Carefully turn out of the tin onto a wooden board.

>8 Dust with icing sugar.

Cut into eight pieces to serve.

chocolate chip cookies

makes 30 cookies

ingredients

175 g/6 oz plain flour
1 tsp baking powder
125 g/4½ oz soft margarine,
 plus extra for greasing
85 g/3 oz light muscovado
 sugar
55 g/2 oz caster sugar
½ tsp vanilla extract
1 egg
125 g/4½ oz plain
 chocolate chips

> **1** Preheat the oven to 190°C/375°F/Gas Mark 5. Lightly grease two baking sheets.

> **2** Place all of the ingredients in a large mixing bowl and beat until well combined.

Serve immediately or store in an airtight container.

>3 Place tablespoonfuls of the mixture on the prepared baking sheets, spacing them well apart to allow for spreading during cooking.

>4 Bake in the preheated oven for 10–12 minutes, or until the cookies are golden brown. Using a palette knife, transfer the cookies to a wire rack to cool completely.

almond biscotti

makes about 35

ingredients

250 g/9 oz whole blanched
  almonds

200 g/7 oz plain flour,
  plus extra for dusting

175 g/6 oz caster sugar, plus
  extra for sprinkling

1 tsp baking powder

½ tsp ground cinnamon

2 eggs

2 tsp vanilla extract

>1 Preheat the oven to 180°C/350°F/Gas Mark 4. Line two baking sheets with baking paper.

>2 Very roughly chop the almonds, leaving some whole.

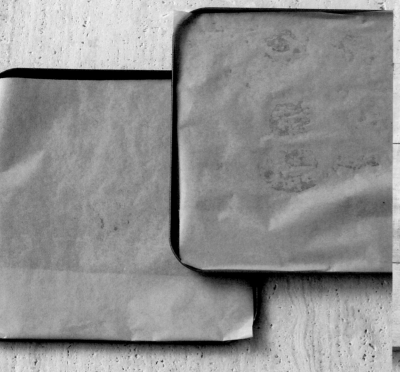

>3 Mix together the flour, sugar, baking powder and cinnamon in a mixing bowl. Stir in the almonds.

>4 Beat the eggs with the vanilla extract in a small bowl, then add to the flour mixture and mix together to form a firm dough.

>5 Turn the dough out onto a lightly floured surface and knead lightly.

>6 Divide the dough in half and shape each piece into a log, roughly 5 cm/2 inches wide. Transfer to the prepared baking trays and sprinkle with sugar. Bake in the preheated oven for 20–25 minutes, until firm.

>7 Remove from the oven and leave to cool slightly, then transfer to a chopping board and cut into 1-cm/½-inch slices. Meanwhile, reduce the oven temperature to 160°C/325°F/Gas Mark 3.

>8 Arrange the slices, cut-sides down, on the baking sheets. Bake in the oven for 15–20 minutes, until dry and crisp. Transfer to a wire rack to cool.

Store in an airtight container to
keep crisp.

crusty white bread

makes 1 loaf

ingredients

1 egg
1 egg yolk
150–200 ml/5–7 fl oz
  lukewarm water

500 g/1 lb 2 oz strong white
  flour, sifted, plus extra for
  dusting
1½ tsp salt

2 tsp sugar
1 tsp easy-blend dried yeast
25 g/1 oz butter, diced
oil, for greasing

> 1 Place the egg and egg yolk in a jug and beat lightly to mix. Add enough water to make up to 300 ml/10 fl oz. Stir well.

> 2 Place the flour, salt, sugar and yeast in a large bowl. Add the butter and rub it in with your fingertips until the mixture resembles fine breadcrumbs.

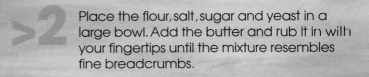

> 3 Make a well in the centre, add the egg mixture and work to a smooth dough. Turn out onto a lightly floured surface and knead well for about 10 minutes, until smooth.

> 4 Brush a bowl with oil. Shape the dough into a ball, place in the bowl, cover and leave to rise in a warm place for 1 hour, or until doubled in volume.

>5 Preheat the oven to 220°C/425°F/Gas Mark 7. Oil a 900-g/2-lb loaf tin. Turn out the dough onto a lightly floured surface and knead for 1 minute until smooth.

>6 Shape the dough so it is the same length as the loaf tin and three times the width. Fold the dough in three widthways and place it in the tin with the join underneath.

>7 Cover and leave in a warm place for 30 minutes, until the dough has risen above the tin.

>8 Place in the preheated oven and bake for 30 minutes, or until firm and golden brown. Transfer to a wire rack and leave to cool.

Cut into thick slices and serve.

pesto & olive soda bread

makes 1 loaf

ingredients
olive oil, for greasing
250 g/9 oz plain flour
250 g/9 oz wholemeal flour
1 tsp bicarbonate of soda
½ tsp salt
3 tbsp pesto
300 ml/10 fl oz buttermilk,
  (approx)
55 g/2 oz pitted green
  olives, roughly chopped
milk, for glazing

>1 Preheat the oven to 200°C/400°F/Gas Mark 6 and line and grease a baking sheet. Sift the flours, bicarbonate of soda and salt into a bowl, adding back any bran from the sieve.

>2 Mix the pesto and buttermilk. Stir in to the flour with the olives, mixing to a soft dough. Add more liquid if needed.

Serve the soda bread on the day of baking.

>3 Shape the dough into a 20-cm/8-inch round and place on the baking sheet. Flatten slightly and cut a deep cross with a sharp knife.

>4 Brush with milk and bake in the preheated oven for 30–35 minutes, until golden brown. The loaf should sound hollow when tapped underneath.

scones

makes 9 scones

ingredients
450 g/1 lb plain flour,
 plus extra for dusting
½ tsp salt
2 tsp baking powder
55 g/2 oz butter
2 tbsp caster sugar
250 ml/9 fl oz milk, plus extra
 for glazing
strawberry jam and clotted
 cream, to serve

>1 Preheat the oven to 220°C/425°F/Gas Mark 7. Sift the flour, salt and baking powder into a bowl. Rub in the butter using your fingertips until the mixture resembles fine breadcrumbs.

>2 Stir in the sugar. Make a well in the centre and pour in the milk. Stir in using a palette knife and bring together to make a soft dough.

Serve freshly baked with strawberry jam and clotted cream.

>3 Turn out the dough onto a lightly floured surface and very lightly flatten it until it is 1 cm/½ inch thick. Cut out scones using a 6-cm/2½-inch biscuit cutter and place on a lined baking sheet.

>4 Brush with a little milk and bake in the preheated oven for 10–12 minutes, until golden and well risen. Leave to cool on a wire rack.

Index